ENTREPRENEURIAL COMPASSION

ENTREPRENEURIAL COMPASSION

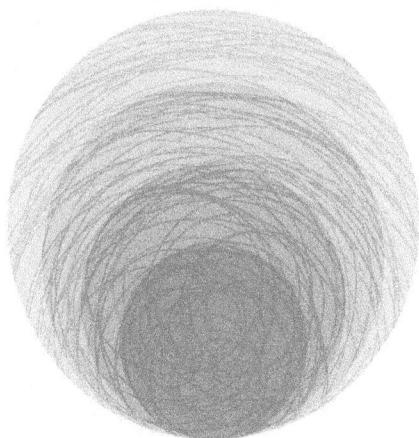

An Entrepreneur's Journey Through

Combat, Suicide, and the Discovery

of Compassionate Leadership

CAL RILEY

CULTURE
T E A M

ENTREPRENEURIAL COMPASSION
*An Entrepreneur's Journey Through Combat, Suicide, and
the Discovery of Compassionate Leadership*

FIRST EDITION

ISBN   978-1-5445-4909-5   *Hardcover*
       978-1-5445-4908-8   *Paperback*
       978-1-5445-4907-1   *Ebook*
       978-1-5445-4906-4   *Audiobook*

For Luke.

CONTENTS

INTRODUCTION

In April, 2013, I was in Afghanistan on what would turn out to be my last deployment. I was in Special Operations Command, and my unit was in the Special Forces compound at our forward operating base. For months, the enemy had been hitting us with indirect fire, trying to get us into our bunkers. When we heard the indirect siren and the computer-generated voice saying, *incoming, incoming, incoming...*, everyone would run into the bunkers—and the enemy knew it.

After months of indirect bombing, they finally attacked. They hit us with the indirect fire first, and everyone went into the bunkers, but this time, suicide bombers breached the walls of the compound. The enemy broke down the walls, and the enemy, wearing suicide vests, ran in through the rubble, got into the bunkers, and blew themselves up.

I wasn't in one of the bunkers that was hit, and many of the bunkers that they ran into were empty that day, but the base was breached, and we were under attack for eight hours. We were taking direct fire from an unfinished hotel across from us. The hotel provided a perfect elevated position with good views over the base, on which the enemy could emplace sniper and machine gun positions. Enemy fire was coming from the direction of the hotel even as the suicide bombers breached the bunkers. The fire coming from that direction was effective, and pretty much everyone on my side of the base had a close call that day—or ten.

One of the other soldiers on the base, Earl Plumlee, earned the Medal of Honor for his actions that day. Plumlee and a couple of other men confronted the bombers head-on and secured almost the entire base on their own.

Six months later, I was at home, working for my dad's construction company.

Less than two years after that, my dad died, and I found myself running the company. I had no construction background, just the leadership experience I brought from the military. I had a newborn son and a team of people relying on me. But I was a fighter. I pushed myself hard, and it paid off.

In 2023, I was at what I thought was the top of my game. The business was doing so well that I'd basically worked myself out of a job. I'd gone from insanely stressful ninety-hour weeks to spending a few hours a week on the business, and it was performing better than ever. I started a coaching business to teach other entrepreneurs. I wasn't just running a successful company. I was telling other people how to run theirs. In less than ten years, I went from Special Operations Command and firefights in Afghanistan to a thriving career as an entrepreneur and coach.

Then, in September of 2023, my brother died by suicide.

His death wrecked my world. A sibling's suicide isn't something you can ever make sense of. There's no "why." It hit me so hard that, right after he died, I didn't know if I would ever go back to my company. My first thought was that I would quit and go to work for a suicide prevention nonprofit. I wanted to do something to make my brother's death meaningful.

I'd spent so long being a "human doing," and suddenly I wanted—I *needed*—to be a "human being."

After a lot of painful reflection, in the midst of the overpowering guilt and sadness I felt after his death, a lightbulb finally came on. Maybe, if my brother had had more compassion in his life, everything would have been different.

So instead of starting something new, or getting involved in work that was already being done, I decided to focus on bringing compassion to my business and to all the people who were already in my life.

I decided to dedicate myself to compassionate leadership—particularly entrepreneurial compassion. Entrepreneurs can be a lot like soldiers. We're driven and dedicated. It can be lonely, isolating work, whether you're running a one-person business or heading a fast-growing company. We tend to tell ourselves that the "human being" work, like compassion and caring for others, is a luxury or a bunch of nonsense. That was the arrogance I had before my brother died, thinking that I knew everything and didn't have to work on myself.

My brother's death has altered my entire life. I will never be the same. And it's still bitterly raw. At the time I'm writing this, it's been less than two years since he died. The lessons I've learned are still fresh, and I know I'm not done learning them.

This book tells the story of what happened when I was forced to rethink everything I thought I knew about leadership and how I treat myself and other people. My one hope for you is that you learn these lessons from me, so you don't have to go through what I went through to get here.

LIFE AS A CIVILIAN

I got out of the military because my wife was pregnant with our first child, my son. When he was born, it was the most incredible, most important moment of my life—and it made me realize I needed to be at home for my family. At the time, my dad was talking to me a lot about joining his company, and I decided it could be interesting to rejoin the family business.

That's all I was thinking, that it would be interesting—something to do while I was figuring out what was next for me. I could never have imagined how the next year would change everything.

In fact, I initially agreed just to manage real estate investments with him, which I thought had potential. I had no interest or desire to work in the business itself. It didn't take long, though, before I ended up working in the construction company because I realized that's where the bread was buttered. That's where the revenue came from that drove everything else, including the real estate investments.

After a few months working for my dad, I took every penny I'd saved up from my multiple deployments and acquired a majority interest in the company. It was a hard choice. Years of military service and careful saving had given me a substantial amount of money, and I had to decide whether to stake it all, everything I'd saved, on buying into the business. I decided it was worth it, and I laid out everything I had.

Technically, that made me the president of the company, but in reality, I was there to start learning, not to take over. My dad had been running the business for more than twenty years, and he was still making all the major decisions. I was not a construction guy. My dad was. He knew the industry. He knew the players. He had the relationships and the expertise. I expected to spend a lot of time learning the ropes from him.

Then, out of the blue, my dad had a stroke that almost killed him. It was clear he was going to be out of commission for a long time. That's when I realized, *oh, man, I've got to figure all this out for myself.* I had never seen the financial year-end close with the company. I didn't know what a P&L or a balance sheet were, or even who our bank was. I didn't know the finances. I didn't know anything about running any business, much less one with two dozen employees, going on thirty years in operation and growing.

Overnight, I was having to make all the major decisions myself, without his guidance. I scrambled, trying to keep the company running while learning everything about keeping a business afloat all at once.

Every day, I was dealing with something I'd never done before, often something I had never even considered as a possibility. A few months after Dad's stroke, I hired an employee and brought him on board—and almost immediately, I got a phone call from someone who had worked with him before. My contact called to inform me that my new hire, who I thought was going to help me run the company one day, was a thief who had embezzled funds from his previous employers multiple times. He was running a scam and had essentially defrauded multiple previous employers of millions of dollars.

I was floored. I had no idea how to handle something like this, so I went to my dad, as usual. But even though he was doing better after the stroke, he'd now also had shoulder surgery and was on pain medication and pretty out of it. He was not in a position to have a productive discussion. I had to make the decision myself.

In the end, I agonized about it for days, but there was only one answer. As hard as it was, I had to let the employee go. I couldn't put the company in jeopardy by keeping him. It was clear he'd run this scam on other businesses, and if I kept him, the likelihood was that he would rob us, too. I'd never fired anybody before, and I hated it. I went over and over it in my mind, wondering whether I'd done the right thing.

A few days later, when my dad was feeling better again and I told him what had happened, I was relieved that he agreed it was the right thing to do. He even joked about it. "Do I still have an office?" he asked. "Did you let me go, too?" I was able to relax a little, knowing he would have done the same thing.

Over the next couple of months, my dad seemed to be making huge strides in recovering from his stroke. I kept going to him with questions. We all thought he was going to be okay and that he'd go back to basically running the business.

Then I got a call from my brother. "Dad's dead," he told me. "You've got to come home."

THROWN INTO THE DEEP END

My dad was an inspiration to me for what it meant to be a compassionate leader. He always put other people first, and it showed. He gave his employees a thirty-three-hour workweek back in the 1990s, before it was trendy. I heard numerous stories about people in the company who he'd given months—almost whole years—fully compensated, to take care of themselves or family members when they were struggling with illness. Loyalty in the company was incredible. You get what you give, and my dad gave everything he possibly could.

When my dad passed away, we had a service for him, and it was packed—standing room only in a huge church. Thousands of people showed up. His kind of caring, his commitment to the idea that people came first, before the company, before profits and revenues, unfortunately seem to a lot of people like a novel concept. And I'm not proud to say that I didn't understand this concept as quickly as I should have, either.

When Dad's service was over and I came back to the business, the new responsibility hit me hard. I didn't know what I was doing, and my mentor was gone. I mean, on one hand, here was my dad, who had been running this business for three years, who'd been in construction for fifty years, and there was me with my one year of experience. He knew the ins and outs of the finances and contracts. He had connections going back decades. I don't even have a construction background. As a kid and a young adult, I'd resisted the idea of going into the family business. I never imagined I would be running it.

How could I possibly take on that burden at the same time I was grieving his loss?

He was supposed to be there to teach me the ropes, to be that resource, and now I didn't have that. I'd been pretty immature up to that point, but that had to change quickly, whether I felt prepared or not. I was in my early 30s, making decisions for my whole family, for the whole company.

It was a crushing level of stress, and I didn't handle it well.

I was overwhelmed, and I was more than a little bit scared. I'd come from the military, where for good or bad, the finances are guaranteed. You know you are getting that check. You know you're going to get paid. It's life and death, there's that risk, but in a strange way it's also secure. The corporate world is the exact opposite. There's not a lot of life-or-death danger, but on the financial side, as an entrepreneur, there's a lot of uncertainty.

Many people think entrepreneurs are like Scrooge McDuck, diving into their limitless pool of coins, and frivolously spending on silly projects, but as nice as that would be, it's just not how it works.

The economists Wesley C. Mitchell and Arthur F. Burns

discovered that a business cycle, on average, is ten years. That means that in any ten years, you'll have two great years, six years that are pretty good, and two years that will almost put you out of business. If we believe we caused the good years, our egos can get out of control, and we could lose the business in the hard years because we will believe that our brilliance was the cause of the success. We have to prepare all the time for those hard years, and we can't get too overconfident during the highs or let the lows throw us into despair or make us give up on the company.

As a green entrepreneur, I didn't know any of that. I had no experience with business cycles. I didn't even know how to recognize what a good year or a bad year looked like. It was a totally different kind of stress and uncertainty from the physical danger I'd signed up for in the military.

So I did what a lot of new entrepreneurs do—I worked a ton of hours, completely unproductively. I was working ninety-hour weeks, and looking back, probably eighty-seven of those hours were doing useless stuff I didn't need to be doing. It went back to that same desire to prove myself that had led me to volunteer to be an Airborne Soldier, then a Ranger, and finally in Special Operations, taking on one of the hardest assignments the military could offer. I wanted to show the people who'd been in my dad's company for years that I could work hard. I spent hundreds of frustrating hours trying to manage every little thing and digging into spreadsheets and details I didn't even understand.

I was directionless. Clueless. Probably my first four years, I didn't have any idea what I was doing.

My team gave me a ton of grace. The people in the company who had worked for my dad told me, "We're here for you." My dad had built his whole life around this compassionate approach, but I didn't see that at the time. Instead of going all in and trusting and caring for my team, I went into full survival mode. My whole life at that time was a combination of pure stress and overreacting to the latest problem.

What I didn't understand then was that compassion was not something that happened without intent. Compassion was a muscle that had to be trained. The work of being compassionate must be as intentional as every other part of the business—and for entrepreneurs, maybe even more so. That's why I'm writing this book—to share with you some specific tools you can use to learn the skill of caring, because let me tell you this: you cannot fake it. If you don't genuinely care, if you don't train that muscle, your team, your clients, and the people you want to work with will know.

You might think that this is an extreme example. Most entrepreneurs won't lose their dad, their mentor, and the person who's been running the company for thirty years all in one terrible moment. But on some level, this is going to happen to you. You're going to experience a level of stress and discomfort in your business that will make it hard for you to be compassionate. The challenge is to take that as an opportunity instead. These are the moments when we grow as people and as leaders.

What I understand now, after learning all of this the hard way, is that you have to prepare to be compassionate, to care for yourself and your business and your team, the same way a strong unit prepares to take care of each other in combat. In this book, I'm going to coach you, from my own difficult experience, on how to maximize your own growth, and the growth of everyone around you, using the tools of compassionate leadership.

GREEN-ON-BLUE

Ft Bragg, North Carolina | Zabul and Ghazni, Afghanistan, 2013

My unit was planning to deploy to Afghanistan, and the big problem on everyone's mind was "green-on-blue" attacks. "Blue" referred to coalition forces: the US and our NATO allies. "Green" referred to our partner forces, including the Afghan National Army, Afghan Local Police, Afghan border police, among others. Green-on-blue refers to situations where our allies, members of the host nation's forces, turn on us and engage us in ambushes, often because they have become ideologically corrupted by the enemy.

Most commonly, this was the result of enemy infiltration into the Afghan forces, especially in the non-Special Operations ranks. The enemy would either recruit disenchanted Afghans already in the ranks or infiltrate units with their own personnel. At the time, there had been 99 reported green-on-blue attacks in Afghanistan, resulting in 152 deaths and 193 injuries among coalition troops and affiliates. There were countless stories of US and NATO officers and NCOs getting shot point-blank in the head by an Afghan ally, groups of US forces getting machine-gunned while at chow or at the gym on the base, and even the use of grenades—all when we had our guard down, and all perpetrated by our Afghan partners behind our own lines.

Obviously, this was a huge problem, not just for safety but for morale. What do you do when the soldiers who are supposed to be your partners, and the people you are supposed to be helping, turn against you?

In military operations, small unit teams use standard operating procedures, or SOPs, to ensure they are doing the key tasks the right way—and doing them the same way every time. The most professional units get so good at operating that they can operate together without a word spoken. They execute these tactics together in training and in combat so often that they know what their teammates are going to do before they even do it.

The TACSOP, or tactical standard operating procedure (TACSOP), is the documentation of those tasks and how to do them, put together in booklet form. It's a manual that fits in your cargo pocket, and it tells you everything the unit does and the way they do it, from clearing a room, to calling in fixed-wing or naval gunfire, to what to do when a vehicle is down and how to cordon off an area for an IED. The most important things, and how you do them as a unit, are all captured in the TACSOP for easy reference. We would have these on us and memorize them, so when we got to the theater during a deployment, we were all on the same page as to how we would operate.

Prior to my team's deployment to Afghanistan, I developed a new battle drill to solve, or at least attempt to mitigate, the "green-on-blue" problem. The concept was that we had to watch each other's backs. The battle drill was based on the theory of 360-degree security. In the military, 360-degree security is essential to the success and survivability of any unit. The "green-on-blue" attacks made this even more critical.

What would happen is that our operators would enter a situation—checking out a building, or even walking into a negotiation—and the enemy would use a feint attack to distract our attention. While everyone was engaged with the feint attack, all looking in one direction, the main attack would commence behind us. I realized that to solve the problem, we had to ensure that at least one operator did not get distracted or look toward the feint attack. We needed to be watching each other's backs at all times.

The battle drill I developed consisted of two operators working together, facing in opposite directions. When we entered a room, whether in the chow hall or an engagement with a key leader off base—outside the wire—we would be facing each other so that we could see over each other's shoulders.

The intent of the drill was to be ready to engage any enemy before he had a chance to take a cheap shot at your comrade while his back was turned.

Before we deployed, we went to the live-fire range and rehearsed this new battle drill. There we were on the range, a few weeks from deploying to Afghanistan, in full kit with our plate carriers, helmets, radios, and weapons, with a full basic load of ammo and smoke grenades, getting ready for "the big mish." We were about to deploy, so we were rehearsing our new battle drill in preparation.

The range was also being used by a training unit with a large group of new recruits who were just starting their training. The trainees would watch us doing the drill and get very confused. You could see them thinking, *What are these guys doing?* To them, it looked like one person on our team was facing the wrong direction. That's because the intent of the drill was to have the discipline not to get distracted by the first contact, but to cover the six o'clock of your battle buddy no matter what. Once the forward-facing operator almost needed a magazine change, only then would the other operator turn and begin engaging the targets. As we made the switch, suddenly the trainees could see what we were up to: covering each other at all times.

This one drill improved morale dramatically. The lesson was, "I'm going to watch your back, and you're going to watch mine, no matter what our rank or position." But even more than that, morale improved because the team knew that we had prepared for this situation, that we had planned in advance, and knew exactly how to handle it.

Most importantly, it was the leader of the team showing

compassion for the men in his unit by saying, "This will not happen to you. Not on my watch."

We never had a single green-on-blue incident on my team. I can't say whether that was because we were ready for it or if we just got lucky, but it never happened to us. What I do know is that whenever soldiers on my team walked into a room or a building, we were always looking over each other's shoulders, watching each other's backs. There was no doubt to anyone in our vicinity that we were prepared for the potential of a surprise engagement by an unforeseen enemy at all times.

I've learned that the same lesson applies as an entrepreneur. As an entrepreneur planning for success, you also plan for what could go wrong and prepare for it. And that has to go beyond planning for the fiscal year or for revenue. Planning for success means showing your team that you care by *preparing for their well-being* just as much as you prepare for profitability.

Compassion is about being intentional and letting your team know that you have their back and that they matter to you as individual human beings.

In fact, I've often thought it would be great if there were a Compassion TACSOP for entrepreneurs, so we could know how to prepare for it and how to be intentional in our caring. So that's what I've tried to put together in this book.

The best units in the world, the most secretive and effective combat units that exist on this planet, have their own TACSOPs, and they use them with their battle drills, rehearsing them over and over and over until they're perfect. I'm not expecting you to become perfect at compassion, but the more you use this book and complete the exercises, the better you'll get at it. My hope is that the book will become a dog-eared, torn-up notebook that sits on your desk because you're consistently referring back to it and applying what you're learning.

QUICK GUIDE

I hope you will read, reflect on, and re-read every word in this book, work through all the exercises, and share them with your team. I also know that entrepreneurs are busy, and a lot of us live with ADHD.

If you don't have time to go through the entire book right now, or if you want a quick guide to hold onto while you're reading, skip to the back of the book. I've laid out a TACSOP for compassion that will give you a place to start.

You can come back for the deeper learning when you have time.

THE SOP FOR COMPASSION

There's no way to lay out exact steps for how to be compassionate in every situation. And there shouldn't be. Compassion is more about mindset than about operations or tactics. In fact, if you take a tactical approach and just do it to get more out of people, it won't work.

But in this book, I will give you concrete action steps you can take to become more compassionate, not just to your team but to yourself, your family, and everyone else you come into contact with. I'll explain why it matters and all the benefits that you and others will get from taking a more compassionate approach. I'll show you how long it took me to get here and how much work I still have to do. I'm far from perfect, and this is a long, ongoing journey.

The good news is that you can get started easily, and even small changes will have big rewards.

Keep in mind as you read this book that caring starts with slowing down. If you're rushing through your day, pushing yourself and everyone around you from one thing to the next, you will not have space for compassion, and it will show. So start by just slowing down every interaction, whenever you can, and taking a minute for yourself and a minute for the other person. Let the relationship come first.

No matter how hard you work at this, there will be times when being compassionate is especially difficult. When you have to have tough conversations, when someone on your team brings up an idea that just won't work, when you get bad news (or even sometimes when you get good news), and when you think you have a good idea or the best solution and just want it implemented right away—you might struggle to find your caring approach in those moments.

I will share stories about all of these situations and offer exercises and guidance for becoming more compassionate even when it's hard.

In order to do this work, you have to be intentional, and being intentional means *planning* to be compassionate. When I take the time to sit down at the beginning of the day and write, "let me be compassionate, let me be inquisitive, let me be curious," and set that intention for how I want to show up, that's when I have great, positive interactions.

Because ultimately, that's what this is about. It's not just about making more money or building your business or having a loyal team, although all of those are great and can come from being more compassionate. This is about what kind of legacy you want to leave in the world.

For me, that legacy is my business. But it's also about something far more personal.

WHY I'M WRITING THIS BOOK

My brother died by suicide in 2023. That's when I started to learn these lessons the hard way and to lead in an entirely new way. I'm hoping, more than anything, that I can spare other people from having to go through what I went through—to help you become more compassionate, and to see why it matters, *before* something like this happens in your life.

These lessons, and the pain of my brother's death, are still very fresh to me. When something that devastating happens, we stop and reevaluate and rethink everything—and those lessons are most powerful when they are raw. Even as I was coping with my brother's death, I knew that I never wanted to forget what it taught me. I wanted to remember everything I was going through so that I could change my life and become a better person. I journaled and wrote down everything I was thinking and learning as I went through it. Those fresh, painful, raw lessons are what I have to offer you, in the hope that you can learn from them, too.

My brother always had two sides to him. He was charismatic and funny—the life of the party. But he could also be moody and angry. When we were kids, he was the chief ruiner of vacations. I have so many pictures of my parents walking next to him, and he would have this pout face on, like he was just angry at the world. I think he experienced life on a highly emotional level. The highs were high, and the lows were low. When things were great, he was amazing to be around, and when things were not great, it was hard to even come near him. He was a fantastic wrestler and a great leader. He was an accomplished lawyer and a veteran of multiple tours of duty.

He was smart, too. He got top marks as an officer in the military, and when he decided to go to law school after my dad died, he became the class president even though he was the oldest person in the class.

I found out in a meeting that he had died by suicide.

I sat there reading that text, not quite knowing how I felt or what to do. Eventually, I got the call and found out that it was true. My dear brother Lucas was gone forever.

My mom didn't know yet, and I knew it was up to me to tell her in person. I went to her house, but she wasn't there. I wasn't sure whether to stay, but then I saw her drive up. As she drove toward me, I pretended to mess with the garage door opener so that she couldn't see my face. It was already unusual for me to be at her house in the middle of the week, and I didn't want her to see me crying and guess why I was there.

I kept my sunglasses on while she parked the car to hide my tears, and then I followed her into the kitchen and asked her to sit down.

Telling her that my brother was gone is one of the hardest things I've ever had to do. My mother is tough. She's someone I really admire. She's been through so much, and she's incredibly resilient, and this hit her hard.

My reaction during that whole time was just numb. I was in shock.

Even now, I have a hard time not blaming myself as his big brother. I know it's not my fault. Lucas had struggled for a long time. His whole life, he wouldn't do any of the normal stuff an adult is supposed to do. He wouldn't go to the doctor or the dentist. He wouldn't take care of himself. He didn't cash his checks from work regularly. I thought that's just what it was like having a little brother. I still don't know if this behavior was related to his death or not.

In the notebook he left behind, he detailed several attempts I didn't know about. He'd quit his job and dramatically decreased his human interaction. He wouldn't pick up the phone or talk to anyone.

He also wrote about how, if his boss had been more under-standing, this wouldn't have happened. Lucas worked as a third-party public defender, working to help mentally ill people not be involuntarily committed. It was emotionally tough work, and he worked from home without any human interaction or support. He'd moved out to the West Coast to start a new life, and he loved it there, but it also meant he was far away from family and other connections.

He wrote that he knew it wasn't his boss's fault, but he had strong feelings about them and about the support he didn't get for doing that hard, emotionally draining work. And that made me think about what I was doing as a boss, how I was showing up for the people who worked for me—and what might be going on in their lives that I didn't know about.

I know my brother's suicide wasn't my fault, as much as I sometimes have a natural inclination to blame myself and to ask what I could have done differently. I know it wasn't his boss's fault. He had a mental illness, and he was isolated. I wasn't the perfect brother. Of course not. Nobody is. I wish my brother was still here. I wish it hadn't happened. But it did. So I had to figure out what to do next.

That's when I started the long, difficult process of seeing myself and the impact I was having on the world, and the people who worked for me, a lot more clearly. I wanted to do something that might help someone else not feel the way my brother did, isolated and alone and unsupported.

What I realized as I started to go through this pain, learning to cope and trying to make sense of this terrible loss, was that I had to start with myself. If I couldn't have compassion for myself as a human being, I wouldn't be able to have compassion for anyone else. And in order to have compassion for myself, I first had to know myself. I had to be willing to honestly and objectively look at how I was treating others and how I was treating myself, and to understand why.

And look, I understand the desire to react against this. I spent a lot of time telling myself, "I'm a combat veteran leader, I don't need therapy," or "I don't have time to be nice, I have a business to run." I told myself that feelings didn't matter, that we were just there to do a job—all the stuff we tell ourselves every day when we don't want to do this tough work of becoming more self-aware.

If you've achieved everything you ever wanted to achieve in your life, and you feel good about your success and about yourself, maybe this doesn't apply to you. But what I've found for myself is that this is applicable every single day because you just don't know what the people around you are going through.

Think about it this way. When you are eighty or ninety years old, lying on your deathbed, you're not going to say, "I wish I'd spent more time at work. I wish we'd gotten that one contract 20 years ago." When we look back on our lives, the things we remember are the people and the relationships and how we made people feel, and what we regret is not spending more time with the people we love.

Entrepreneurs can be especially bad about this. We're very driven people, always telling ourselves, *If I could just do this one more thing*... But there will always be the next thing, and the next thing. There will always be more to acquire and do and achieve. The good news is, we can walk and chew gum at the same time. You can have both.

If there's one thing to take away from this book, it's that message: you can have both. You can achieve the things you want to achieve *and* have compassion. You can achieve all your goals *and* have a fantastic family life, self-compassion, and a great culture at your company.

As a public defender who worked with tireless dedication to help people with mental illness not become involuntarily committed, the work my brother was doing definitely had an impact on him, and it didn't help that he worked remotely. He worked all day on a computer in his apartment, disconnected from the world.

The research tells us that people historically needed about two times as much positive feedback as critical feedback to feel positive about themselves and their relationships. In the army, I learned the term "shit sandwich" for this. The bottom slice of bread was a positive statement, then the meat of "constructive feedback" in the middle was the "shit," and then you rounded it off with another positive statement at the end to top off the sandwich. A lot of people have heard this approach, and it's not the worst way to give feedback. But in our current working environment, with all of the changes in technology and the fact that we are working more remotely now than ever, the amount of positive feedback people need has gone up a lot. In the remote environment, people don't need twice as much positive to negative—they need *seven* times as much. That remote work disconnection had a big effect on my brother, and it's part of why compassion is even more important now than ever.

I know in my heart that if this kind of compassion had been available to my brother, if someone at work had shown greater care for him, he would still be here today. Unfortunately, we seem to be going in the other direction. We're disregarding the need to care deeply about the people around us, and that's a wrong this book is intended to right.

I'm ashamed that it took my brother's death for me to truly adopt these principles of caring and compassion. That's why I chose to write this book: to honor my brother's memory and to try to increase the compassion that others feel in their lives and work. All the proceeds for the book will go to helping stop soldier and veteran suicide, but the potential impact goes far beyond soldiers to everyone you interact with in your life, your family, and at work—and yourself, too.

IT HAS TO START WITH YOU

After my brother died, and as I started to see how far I'd gotten from the compassionate and caring leadership my father modeled, the first hurdle was to learn to forgive myself. For better or worse, that's how people learn. Sometimes the only way to get experience is to get experience.

People learn, not by thinking how great they are at something, but by realizing, "I'm not good at this," or "I'm not doing this well." Before I could start on the path to being more compassionate to others, I had to start with compassion for myself.

And that's not just important because it allows you to learn from your mistakes. You have to start with self-compassion because what the leader does, the leadership team will do, and then the whole company will do it, and it will start to spread on its own. It will become a culture of compassion that drives loyalty, commitment, and effectiveness, and also humor and enjoyment.

HOW TO USE THIS BOOK

Reading this book is a great starting place to build compassion into your life and your leadership—but it's not the end of the journey. After every chapter, you'll see exercises to build your own compassion practice.

These are not exercises I got from a workshop or made up

out of nowhere. This is the work I do myself. Whether it's stepping back and understanding why I'm so invested in a particular outcome or course of action, or taking the time to be grateful for the people in my life, these exercises are how I stay grounded in, and true to, my commitment to be more compassionate to myself and others.

I recommend that you stop at the end of each chapter and give yourself time to complete the exercise. Don't just think about the answer; **get yourself a specific notebook for your compassion practice and keep all your notes and exercises in it.** As you complete the activities, that notebook will become your own, personalized roadmap to better, more caring leadership.

Before you head to Chapter 1, **take a few minutes, in a quiet space, to reflect on your current leadership by taking the Entrepreneurial Compassion Self-Assessment** on the next page. You might be surprised what it tells you about where you need to start work—and what you're already doing well.

If you want, you can head over and take the Self-Assessment on my website at calriley.com.

Becoming a more compassionate leader has been one of the most important journeys of my life, and I hope you can find ways to incorporate these lessons into your own life—at work and beyond.

ENTREPRENEURIAL COMPASSION SELF-ASSESSMENT

	1 2 3	4 5 6	7 8 9	10 11 12	SCORE
Self-Talk	I often put myself down or use negative language about myself. Sometimes people hear me do this, or mention it to me.	I'm aware of my negative self-talk, but I'm not sure what to do about it. It keeps slipping into my thinking and my speech.	I've made a strong effort to reduce my negative self-talk and be kind to myself, even if I make a mistake. I'm making progress.	I've made substantial progress in how I speak to myself, and I still self-reflect on it and even help others speak more kindly to themselves.	
Self Awareness	I don't have time for self-reflection. I have a business to run. Self awareness doesn't seem valuable to my work or my life.	I know that self-reflection and understanding how my patterns affect myself and others would be helpful, but I don't have the time or energy.	I take the time to reflect on my own behaviors and thought patterns regularly, and I use what I've learned about myself to improve my leadership.	Self-reflection is a major part of how I lead and how I relate to others, in my business and in my life. It drives my growth as a person.	

	1	2	3	4	5	6	7	8	9	10	11	12	SCORE
Awareness of Others	People come to work to do a job. It's not my business to know about their personal lives, and I'm sure they don't want to know about mine.			I would like to have better and deeper relationships with the people around me, but I'm already overburdened.			I've started building deep and authentic relationships with the people on my team. I care about who they are as people, and they know it.			Deep and authentic relationships are the building blocks of a successful and meaningful business. Building those relationships is a major part of my job as a leader, and I'm always working on them.			
Core Values	I work on whatever needs to be done at the moment. I pursue whatever clients or opportunities come my way. Talking about core values seems like a distraction.			Doing work that's personally meaningful to me and is in line with my values would be nice, but it doesn't feel realistic when the day-to-day running of the business takes up all my time and effort.			I have spent time defining my core values and understanding how my business and my leadership fit with them. I choose projects and business strategies that are in line with and support what's most important to me.			Core values drive not only my own leadership and decision making, but also my relationships with my team. We have discussed and agreed on our shared values, and we live and work by them.			
Curiosity Mindset	When things don't go the way they're supposed to, I immediately look for who's responsible. I don't waste time asking why they did it, I just want to make sure it never happens again.			I know that people on my team might be struggling, or our communication might not be great, but it's more important to keep things moving forward, even if that means just telling people what to do.			When something doesn't go the way I planned or hoped it would, I stop and get curious. I ask genuinely curious questions and rarely ask questions that are actually statements.			Curiosity is a cornerstone of how I live my life and lead my company. I am always learning how to ask better questions and fully listen to the answers and not simply wait for my turn to speak. I embrace the silence of a conversation.			

	1	2	3	4	5	6	7	8	9	10	11	12	SCORE
Trust Mindset	I find it difficult to believe that people will do what they say they'll do unless I'm on them all the time. I haven't taken a vacation in years because I need to be present for anything to get done.			I wish I could take more vacations or spend less time overseeing people and making sure work is getting done. But taking the time out to teach people, or to learn new delegation techniques, will have to wait until I'm less swamped.			I've put in a lot of effort to develop trust with my team. I know the difference between tasks and projects that I, as the entrepreneur, need to be involved in, the tasks I can completely leave to others, and the tasks that can serve as trust-building opportunities.			The trust between me and my team is so well developed that I only attend a few meetings. I spend most of my time working on opportunities that excite me.			
Investment in the Team	I built this business. Any profit is generally reinvested into the business, or belongs to me. I may give bonuses sometimes, but it's not part of my strategic planning, and it's an "extra."			I give bonuses when I can, but right now, the business needs all the investment it can get. And I need to put aside money for hard times. You never know what might happen.			Investing in the people who work for me is part of my annual strategic planning. They make the business work, and it's important to me to recognize their contribution and invest in them.			I invest in and reward those around me. I understand that the return on this investment will be exponential because I've seen it time and time again.			
Greater Good	I have a gut feeling that there is a lot of conflict in my company because I don't want to deal with it. I don't have the time, or I'm afraid of what will happen if I have the tough conversations: it might be awkward, or the person might quit.			I know I tend to avoid conflict, and there are ongoing issues that need my attention for the company to be at its best. But I keep putting them off, or else I just don't have time to deal with them. Something always seems to come up.			I give people the benefit of the doubt, but I make time for and prioritize the tough conversations that I need to have. I know that having those conversations will be for the greater good of the company in the long run.			I've had so many tough conversations that I've gotten good at them. I have them with my leadership team as needed, and they have them with members of their own teams. Our ability to tackle hard topics drives our growth and our culture.			

	1	2	3	4	5	6	7	8	9	10	11	12	SCORE
Letting Go	Everything in the business is important, so I have to be involved in all of it. Nothing leaves the building until I've signed off on it.			I regularly do tasks that I'm not great at and that someone else should be doing, but I struggle to give up anything, especially if it's something I can do faster than I could teach it.			I regularly commit time to reviewing the work I'm doing and asking what I need to control and what I can let go. I'm able to let other people take the lead, and I ask questions more than I talk most of the time.			I lead a team of experts who know their work better than I do. I'm happy to let them manage their own projects so that I can focus on areas where I add value. Others throughout the company are able to do the same.			
Authentic Relationships	This is a business. People are here to do a job. Caring about them isn't part of the job description, and it's not something I have time for. To the extent that people do care, it's performative or just for show.			Showing my team that I deeply care about them would be nice, but there just isn't time in the day.			I intentionally make time to show the people on my team that I care about them authentically. I regularly reflect on and set intentions around doing this better.			Deep and authentic caring is the basis of our company culture. My team knows that I have their back, and they authentically care about the business and its success. I also see examples of authenticity every day in my employees' engagements with clients and with each other.			

Score yourself from 1–12 in each of the areas above, then take a few minutes to write down your reactions. What surprised you? What areas might you work on first? Where are you already showing authentic compassion?

Make a plan to improve one score this quarter and write it here:

Consider retaking the assessment after you've read the book and see what's changed. Then come back in six months and track your progress.

Remember, developing compassionate entrepreneurship is a continuous learning process. Your self-assessment is likely to change over time. Self-awareness and intentional reflection are the first steps toward growth.

DISCOVERY EXERCISE: IMPACTFUL MOMENTS

When my son was born, my entire life changed overnight. My priorities, my decisions, the way I thought about the future—nothing would ever be the same. Seeing my son for the first time was the greatest moment I've ever experienced.

My brother's death also changed me, in ways I'm still trying to understand. I see and relate to other people radically differently than I did before he died.

Good or bad, there are moments in your life that have an impact that far, far outweighs the rest. When these moments are fresh and raw, you can see things clearly that you couldn't see before. Over time, the impact fades, and the lessons settle in and become the way you live your life, but in those days or months, or even years, following an event that changes everything, you rethink all the ideas you thought defined you.

That's one of the reasons I'm writing this book now: to share with you what I've learned while it's still clear and fresh in my mind, in the hope that it will impact you, too.

Before we get into the definition of compassion and the details of what I've learned, take a moment to think about your own most impactful moments.

What have been the moments or events in your life that have changed your perspective, or the way you approach the world, permanently? How fresh or raw are they? Have some of them "sunsetted," so that they no longer impact you in the same way?

My brother's death was, and is, a terrible loss. Nothing can change that. I would never, ever say that it was good for me. But I have to find a way to take something positive out of it, or the negatives and the pain will be too much. I have to find a way to live with it and make some sense out of it.

In this book, I ask you to look at yourself and your own

experiences with that same kind of clarity and ask yourself, "What is the right thing to learn from this? How can this really great, or really terrible, or difficult or wonderful, experience serve me in the future—and how can I use it to serve others?"

I've learned that I didn't have to abandon my life and work for a nonprofit. I could use my business, and my leadership, to spread compassion and connect more deeply with the people around me. I hope that this book helps you see how you can use your life, and your company, and your leadership to do the same.

1

WHY COMPASSION MATTERS

Euphrates River, Southwest Baghdad, Iraq: 2006

The mission went wrong from the second the Chinook set us down. It was one of my earliest missions as a Platoon Leader, and I was sure I'd planned everything down to the last detail. I'd gathered my platoon together and completed mission planning, pre-mission checks and inspections, and our rehearsals, and I felt like we were on the same page.

Our job was to recover a missing soldier. The story we were told was that, in a previous deployment—before we arrived—a unit was doing mounted operations at night. They had three Humvees with turrets, and the soldier in the middle turret fell asleep. The assumption was that the enemy snuck up on his position and kidnapped him, and he had not been recovered. In other words, he was DUSTWUN (Duty Status–Whereabouts Unknown): no one knew exactly what happened to him, or whether he was alive.

By the way, this mission, and all the other missions I was part of during my time in Special Operations, took place twenty years ago. And who knows, maybe they told us this story to scare the shit out of us about not falling asleep on patrol. Either way, we knew that a soldier from a previous deployment had gone missing, and it was our job to find him. Or more likely, his remains.

Almost as soon as the Chinook touched down in the pitch black at two in the morning, the mission hit chaos and never recovered.

Hold on, though. I'm getting ahead of myself.

Going into this mission, I was sure I had a great plan, probably the best plan I'd developed in my few years in the military. This was the plan of all plans! I knew that what we were doing was high stakes. It was an air assault mission, which meant we'd be inserted in by helicopters. Plus, it was a battalion-level operation, with over one thousand personnel involved. All eyes were on this mission. This was 2006 Iraq, and we were being inserted into an area that had been untouched by coalition forces for years. We were based in the Sunni Triangle, the so-called "triangle of death," an area with tons of enemy activity and littered with improvised explosive devices. We had to be ready.

We'd already spent weeks taking over command from the outgoing unit. We had executed left-seat, right-seat rides, a gradual transition from one unit to the next. We'd ride around in the right seat, the passenger seat, watching and learning from the outgoing unit. We saw how they did everything, from IED clearing, to pulling security at the Patrol Base and Observation Posts, to cleaning the toilets. The first time through, we just rode along and watched. Then we'd switch, and our new unit would be in the driver's seat, with the outgoing soldiers sitting in the passenger seat, giving feedback. Then they left, and we were in charge.

I was pretty new to command, and a battalion-level air assault into dangerous territory was a big deal, so I worked hard. I went through all the field manuals and researched the best way to tackle the mission. I put together a strategy, laid out all the tactics, presented it to my team, and rehearsed it in detail. We practiced it, perfected it. And I thought I had buy-in from my platoon.

The night of the mission, forty of us loaded into the Chinook and took off. The desert can be 130 degrees during the day, but at night the temperature drops fast. It was probably in the 60s, but it felt colder after the intense heat of the day. The ramp pulled up, blocking out the wash from the propellers, and we lifted off. There was a lot of tension, everybody thinking about what we needed to do.

Just before we landed, I put on the headset that enabled me to listen in to the pilots, and I was hit with the loudest heavy-metal music I've ever heard in my life, just pounding, screaming music, and then a guy started counting, yelling out numbers as fast as he possibly could. I was still trying to figure out what was going on when we landed.

Everything moved quickly from there. The bird touched down, the ramp opened…and I stepped off and fell ten feet straight into a ravine—immediately followed by the other thirty-nine soldiers in my platoon. We were using a concept in infantry tactics called noise and light discipline. When exercising noise and light discipline, everyone works to absolutely limit any noise or light, which is perfect in theory. In retrospect, it sure would have been smart for me to break the rules just this once with a quick check with the taclight (the mini flashlight attached to my rifle) on my M-4 rifle to see if we were landing in a canal or a pit…or the ravine we landed in. But that's how experience works, I guess. You get it after you do it. So there we were in a ravine, piled on top of each other, trying to set up some kind of security, which is nearly impossible when you're in a human Jenga jigsaw puzzle.

We were carrying food, water, weapons, night vision goggles, batteries, ammunition, grenades, rucksacks—close to a hundred pounds of gear each. Plus, night vision only works when there is ambient light around for it to amplify. On a cloudy night in the desert, it's like walking around blindfolded, and even when there is enough ambient light for the night vision to work properly, there's a strange, ambient green glow to everything that decreases your depth perception and makes it hard to judge distances and to know where you are in space. We were scrambling in this green-lit blindness, flailing in what felt like a pile of arms and legs, dragging all this gear and feeling exposed and unsafe.

In a mission like this, morale is the most important thing. If everyone is working together, feeling like the mission is going well, and is set on the goal, everything comes together. If not, if morale is lost, it's often the start of one thing going wrong after another.

Morale was shot from the moment we landed in that ravine, and it did not get better.

After that chaotic start, my NCOs (the non-commissioned officers in my platoon working under me) basically changed everything I'd planned. Everything we had rehearsed, all the stuff they'd agreed to, they just decided, *nope*, and on the spot changed where everyone was going to go. All I could think was that my plan was being shot down by my own platoon.

It was only decades later, after my brother died, that I was able to see this incident more clearly. I thought for years that my platoon just straight-out disobeyed me because they didn't like me. I took it personally, and I was furious. I didn't have enough experience, or enough perspective, to see that, actually, my plan was shot by the terrain. It wasn't what we'd thought it was on the map, and that changed the mission.

Instead of reacting to that new information, I was telling myself, "We all agreed this plan (my plan!) was the best plan. How could they do this to me? How could they be telling me that this plan I'd worked on so hard was no good?" My attitude wasn't to ask questions or to find out why they wanted to change the plan. I expected them to obey me and follow my orders without taking their experience into account, and that made the tension even worse.

After we established security, I did a quick leader's recon with my long-range night vision equipment, and the first thing I saw was fires burning out in the distance. I turned to my Platoon sergeant and told him we needed to go investigate that, to figure out what it was.

He looked at me like I was nuts, and said, "No way are we doing that, that's crazy." He flat-out refused.

The situation wasn't what we'd planned for. Falling into a hole, having the NCOs question me, arguing about whether to investigate the fires—everything was going sideways. So even once we managed to secure off a building and started to review the plan, suddenly they didn't agree with that anymore, either. *No way*, they said. *That's not going to work.*

Long story short: we didn't find the soldier we were looking for. We came across one spot where the cadaver dog alerted, but it was a gravesite of little stillborn babies. After that, morale was shot for real.

And it just went from bad to worse. We took multiple casualties from dismounted IEDs that were buried in the desert. We'd been basically led into this area by a local national who purported to know where the DUSTWUN body was buried.

Instead, the local national tricked us into an area where half a dozen of my guys took shrapnel. No one died—thank God—but it was a terrible lesson in trust, and when not to trust.

That's the reality of war. Not every mission is a success. Hard things, terrible things even, are going to happen.

But that wasn't the problem. The problem was me. I was pissed about my platoon sergeant disobeying me in front of my team. I took everything they did personally. What did I expect to happen? I had never shown them the compassionate leadership they needed to be successful, for them to trust me, or for us to work together.

When I was planning for the mission, I went to the books, I put together a plan that sounded good to me, I briefed my team, and I said, "This is what we're doing." I got no buy-in. I took zero time to find out who these people were, their families, their goals, their feelings. These soldiers were going to be executing the plan, keeping me and each other safe, and I acted like they didn't matter except as tools to get my perfect plan done.

Then, when things went south, I took it personally. When they told me the plan we'd put together wouldn't work, or that we shouldn't go out and investigate the fires, I took it as an affront. Military culture is very macho—especially in the infantry, and especially in an Airborne Infantry Platoon—and I just took that macho culture and ran with it. I promoted it. I told everybody what we were doing and didn't ask a single question. I didn't care about knowing my team. Everything was about my plan and about me as the leader.

So when things went wrong, I didn't have the rapport with them to get it back on track. We had no trust in each other. I'd just taken my idea and rammed it down their throats without out a second's thought that these were intelligent, experienced people who might have their own insights about how to do this incredibly dangerous mission we were about to do together. They did not feel that I cared about them, so instead of attacking the problem, we attacked each other. There was nothing, no relationship, to fall back on. I did not show compassion for them as human beings, and the result was that they didn't care about my plan, my mission, my goals, or anything else I needed from them.

In retrospect, what happened on that mission was a lightbulb moment for me. Everything I did to get ready for that mission—all the planning and reading and preparing and practicing—all that stuff was pointless without letting them know that I really cared.

That can't just be "another thing." It's the *only* thing. If that's not there, we fail.

I led troops in combat for ten years in the global war on terror. I've led over seven hundred combat patrols. Since I got back, I've led people in the corporate world, both as an entrepreneur myself and as a coach for other business leaders and entrepreneurs.

I'm not perfect, but I've been doing this work for a long time, and I have learned one thing over and over again. If there is no goodwill, nothing else will matter. If your people don't know you care about them—truly, authentically care about them—your ninety-hour work weeks and your perfectly planned strategy won't make any difference.

Can you succeed without compassion? Sure. But it will be a constant effort of pushing upstream. You'll be just like me on that mission, expending unnecessary energy forcing everyone around you to conform to the plan. Even worse, when you go home at night after being a freight train all day, it's hard to turn it off. It affects everyone in your life, starting with you.

With compassion, everything turns around. You build trust,

and that means you can let the people on your team use their own intelligence to get the work done. You develop relationships, which means people are in your corner when things go wrong—which they will. You care about the people you work with and want them to succeed, which makes you feel good about going to work. You go home to your family less exhausted, less frustrated, and more loving.

Your business becomes more successful. That's important. But at the same time, it starts to be about something more than just making money. It becomes your legacy. You create something that transcends everything else: lasting and genuine relationships that people will never forget, and a company that is a source of good that will live on even after you're gone.

The question, then, is this: if compassion can do so much for us as leaders, for our teams, and for our businesses, why aren't we doing it already?

THE SUPERHERO COMPLEX

Sometimes I think about that scene in *Indiana Jones* where the crowd parts, and a swordsman starts swirling his sword around, showing off his skills, preparing to fight Indy, getting ready for a classic, over-the-top fight scene—and instead, Indiana Jones just rolls his eyes, takes out his pistol, shoots him, and walks away.

Many people think that military work is like the showy swordsman: flashy fist fights and exaggerated superhuman skills. It's not. It's much more like what Indy did—what's the simplest and best way to accomplish the objective? We're humans. We've got families to go back to. It's never about how elaborate we can be. There are no moments like those scenes in the movies when fifty trucks suddenly arrive out of nowhere, there's a quick and decisive gunfight, and everyone is surprised and then gets to look cool and show off. The truth is, if fifty trucks are coming from somewhere, you probably know hours in advance, if not days or weeks. The best military work is done when you figure out the simplest way to do something and then do it well. (In fact, there's a saying in the Army that the boss you want is the one who's smart and lazy. We'll get back to that in detail in Chapter 2.)

But so often, as entrepreneurs and as leaders, we act like the swordsman. For a long time, that was me. I felt like there was a nobility in saying, "Look how much work I'm doing! Look how hard I'm working!" I was swirling those swords around as fast as I could. It was like I needed the team to see me doing too much, like that would push them to be just as invested.

The reality, though, is that your team is going to see that for what it is. They're going to know you can't keep it up forever, and they're going to feel like you're more invested in showing how much you work than in seeing, leading, or caring about them.

No matter who you are, no matter how smart you are or what a great plan you have or how much experience you've got, you will not get very far alone. And when you don't care about people, when you don't start with compassion, you will be alone. Even if you're surrounded by people, you're alone because none of them are really with you. None of them care about what you want. That's what happened to me on that mission in Iraq. I was surrounded by people—supposedly my own team, my own unit—and I was alone.

The route to success, the way to turn this around, is compassion.

WHAT IS COMPASSION?

Let's start with what compassion *isn't*.

Most importantly, compassion isn't faking an interest in people to get something out of them. In the military, we had a joke that you could see high-ranking officers visiting, walking around, asking, "Where you from, son?" They'd ask that to everybody they talked to. And whatever the soldier answered, the higher-up would find some connection. If the soldier said he was from Texas, he'd come back with, "Oh, yeah, I've got a cousin in Houston," or something like that, and move on.

They didn't really care about the answer. They were just looking for something they could say to seem like they'd made a connection.

Anybody can see through that. They might expect it or even forgive it—after all, the higher-up is only there for the day, and he's busy—but they are not fooled. And it doesn't buy any loyalty or commitment from them, because it's completely transactional. They're giving you just the amount of attention that they think will buy your loyalty or your hard work.

As entrepreneurs, we're under the same kinds of pressures. It can feel like we don't have the energy or the time to genuinely connect with every person on our team. We spend thirty seconds asking about the family before jumping into what we really came for, which is what we need from them. Your team will give you a lot of grace. They'll believe that you're busy and don't have time to show a deeper interest.

But they will know, on a deeper level, that you don't actually care.

Compassion also isn't "work-life balance." Work-life balance is a term that sounds nice. It's a catchy phrase, and a lot of companies use it to seem friendly and authentic. But it's a false authenticity. What it really means is, "You need to balance your life to fit into my work." Work-life balance implies that there should be a balance between work and your life—between your job and the things that matter most, like your life, your health, and your relationships.

Work and life shouldn't be balanced. Life should come first. People, family, health, the things that matter to you, the impact you have on people: those things should be more important. Work should take a secondary position to life and wellbeing.

We do work to support what matters to us, not the other way around.

So if compassion isn't acting nice to get what you want from people, and if it's not work-life balance, what is it?

Compassion is deeply and authentically caring about others in an intentional and present way.

Being authentic means that you actually care. It's not a strategy or a tactic. It's a deep, honest desire to know about and support the people around you.

Being intentional means you are prepared to work on this, to put in time and effort to get there. It's not easy or simple to bring authentic compassion to yourself or to others. It's especially difficult when things go wrong, when someone messes up, when circumstances are hard. So compassion requires you to act intentionally, to *decide* to be more caring, to take action on it, to assess how you're doing, and to keep trying.

Being present means putting the entire focus of your attention on making a connection to a human being and actually and deeply caring about them. That connection might be with yourself or with someone else, but either way, you are focused completely on it, not thinking about what you wanted to say next or what you need to get done today. You're not just waiting for your turn to talk. You're present with them, one human being to another.

DOES IT REALLY MATTER?

There are going to be a lot of stories in this book about people I've led, people who have been on my teams in the military and as an entrepreneur, or people I've coached. But I've also experienced the difference compassion makes from the other side.

When I was in Iraq, about a year in, I got a message telling me that my mom was sick. She'd had a life-altering, almost life-ending stroke. She had almost died, and I was called home to be there for my family, and for her.

I went home and spent the time I needed with my family. And when I got back to Iraq, I found out I wasn't a Platoon Leader anymore. I'd been "promoted" to S3 Air staff officer. It was like a punch in the gut. I won't go into the specifics of military jobs, but this wasn't a good assignment to get after being a Platoon Leader. I'd worked my ass off to get promoted, and now I'd been given this other role. It felt like a punishment for going home.

It was a rough time. I was stressed out, worried about my mom, thinking about my family—and now I have to accept that all my hard work isn't going to pay off the way I expected, and felt I deserved. My career suddenly felt like it was at a standstill, along with everything else.

As a tough-guy Infantry Officer, though, I knew I couldn't get visibly upset. I'd been assigned to a new boss as part of the new assignment, and one day when I was really having a rough time, this boss, sensing my distress, called me into his office, closed the door, looked me right in the eye, and and said, "I do not care about you."

You might think this would have surprised me, but by that time, I knew him well enough that it was pretty much exactly what I expected.

What you need to understand is that the military, especially combat units, do not know what to do with any feeling other than anger. So the sum of all military combat training is to find that anger and use it. You learn to take all your other feelings and either turn them into anger or suppress them.

If you've ever seen the movie *Talladega Nights*, you might remember the scene with Ricky Bobby (Will Ferrell) and Cal Naughton, Jr. (John C. Reilly), when Cal asks Ricky if he might be allowed to win some of the races. Ricky says, "But if you won, how am I gonna win?" Cal thinks it over and says, "Yeah, I'll just bury it down inside." He and Ricky laugh, and Ricky says, "Bury it deep down in there, and never bring it up again!"

That's what you learn in the military. The Army doesn't know what to do with other feelings—hence the staggering suicide epidemic that this book is hoping to put a dent in. It probably had something to do with my brother's suicide, too. My brother never spoke to me very much about his service, but I assume he experienced the same kind of "emotional training" I did.

So when my boss said he didn't care about me, I wasn't surprised. It's the military, and that's what you expect from that culture. I acted professionally, and I did my job.

That's all I did, though: exactly what I was supposed to do.

I did everything I could for my team. But for him, I wasn't going to do anything extra. I did not care about performing for him because he didn't care about me. End of story.

Then I got a new leader. Suddenly, I found myself working my butt off. I would have done anything for him, and when I look back on it, all he did differently was genuinely care. He cared about me. He wanted me to succeed. He trusted my intelligence. He'd tell me what the operational objective was, then let me figure out how to get it done. He wanted to know how I was feeling. He joked around and got to know everyone who worked for him, and showed all of us that he genuinely cared about us.

The part that really gets me is what happened when the first boss was on his way out. He had to do an evaluation of me before he left, and he said to me, "You're doing a much better job for this guy than you ever did for me. Whatever you've changed about yourself, keep it up. It would have been great if you had done that well when I was your boss. I don't need to know what changed or care, but keep it up." That was it. Not once did he consider that his own behavior might have affected my performance. He didn't ask me what he could have done to get this higher level of success out of me. He had no curiosity at all about what had changed, or about me as a person.

The answer, if he had been interested, was simple: one leader cared, the other one didn't. That totally changed the way I performed.

That's where this journey toward compassion starts: with understanding how much you impact people. That first leader missed out on an incredible opportunity to improve himself, to get better performance out of people, to enjoy his work more, and to feel connected—all because he couldn't, or wouldn't, see the ways his own lack of compassion was the problem.

Human connection is exceptionally important. People who are in solitary confinement go crazy after a surprisingly short period of time. Nothing else in your business, or in your life, is as potentially powerful as human connections and relationships. That's as true in leadership as it is in your family and with yourself. Without those connections, even the best strategies and plans can fail.

When you bring authentic compassion, the opposite happens. Suddenly, you have to work a lot less to get the same results because trust, rapport, and commitment drive performance. Instead of having to sit on everyone all day to get things done, people want to work hard for you because you care about them.

If you're still in doubt about whether compassion matters, just ask your team. If they think they could perform better, if they think the company would be better, if they know that they would be more committed to the mission and the work, if you were more compassionate, then you've got your answer.

And if you're not willing to ask your team that question, I think you've got an answer there, too.

A DIFFERENT OUTCOME

It was almost the end of my time in Iraq, and we were on another air assault mission, this time in Blackhawk helicopters. We had a list of ten high-value targets, and our job was to raid a house and find the enemy and take them out. Once again, it was a high-stakes mission in the middle of the night, from helicopters, with no assurance of success.

Despite the similarities, this time everything went differently.

After that first mission, I had learned my lesson, and I'd spent the ten months between the two missions developing compassion, trust, and presence with my team. I got to know them. I found out who they were as people outside of their jobs in my unit. I invested in them and their success.

I went on as many patrols as I possibly could, hundreds of dismounted patrols, walking beside them and carrying as much of the load as I could. I did so many night patrols that my solar watch died. I had to get a second one so I could leave one in the sun while I was doing day and night missions.

I started giving my team credit when things went well and taking the blame when they went wrong.

Over time, the way they responded to me started to shift. There was more respect—and there was also a lot more fun. I could relax, because the more I got to know them, the more I trusted their ability to get things done. We could joke and get to know each other as human beings.

And this time, when I got the orders for the mission, I included them in the planning. I got the leaders on my team together and asked them what they thought. We set up chairs in the middle of the patrol base, lined up the way we'd be sitting on the Blackhawk, and practiced how we would get out. We created a terrain model and a mock-up of the structures where we would conduct our raid, and used an empty building to rehearse our mission at the platoon level, all the way down to fire team level. We prepared for everything that could go wrong.

On the night of the mission, it was hot and windy. The sand was blowing everywhere. But when we landed, we knew exactly what we were doing. We exited the helicopters with speed and, per our plan, we breached the doors to the building. The first teams were in quicker than we had rehearsed, and we had the whole site secured with an aerial quick reaction force in blocking positions to get any squirters in mere minutes. (Squirters is a military term for enemies that run away during a raid.) We collected sensitive data we needed, exploited the site, and were ready at exfil—to exfiltrate, or leave the objective—in record time.

Just as the birds were about to land, I saw a few of my team go back into the building we'd just cleared and exfiled, and I asked my PSG, "What are they doing?" He said, "They forgot a spare barrel bag."

Even though we had a great plan and everything was well rehearsed and I had the buy-in and compassion, we still messed up. Granted, this was nothing compared to the massive fuckup of the first mission, but still it wasn't perfect. The point is: don't sacrifice progress at the altar of perfection. The first mission had gone wrong from the first moment and never got better, and as a result, it took much longer than we expected. This time, it took us half as long as we'd planned.

In the end, it was an absolute success because of the rapport and trust we had built, and because of the preparation we put into it.

Compassion is the same way. You have to prepare for it. During the months between those missions, I didn't sit around hoping they would learn to trust me. I had meaningful conversations with each and every one of them, conversations where I was truly present. I had to learn how to do that. I had to learn not to just wait my turn to say what I wanted, but to actually hear them and listen to them and learn about them. I had to show them that I meant it, that I was trustworthy.

Every time I had an important conversation with one of them, I had to prepare for that, too.

Maybe there are people who are just naturally 100% compassionate toward everyone. This book isn't for them. That's not how it was for me. I had to learn, first, that it mattered. Then I had to understand what it really meant to be compassionate. I had to practice and fail and practice some more. For that matter, I'm still practicing. By no means am I perfect at this, or finished learning.

And the first thing I had to learn was that, no matter what team I was working with, or what the mission was, if I wanted to be authentically compassionate, I had to start with myself.

DISCOVERY EXERCISE: EGO INVESTMENT

When my NCOs decided not to follow my plan, I couldn't see that the terrain wasn't what we expected. I couldn't see that they were reacting to the change in the reality around us. I was sure they were disrespecting me in front of my platoon.

My ego was way over-invested in getting one specific result, and in being "in charge" and getting what I thought was respect from my NCOs. Actually, what I wanted wasn't just respect but obedience. I didn't have the respect for them, or the trust in them, to stop and listen to their assessment of the changed landscape and mission.

Self-awareness is the first step to compassion, and self-awareness starts with the ability to step back and notice when your behavior isn't serving the team or the outcome. All too often, for all of us as entrepreneurs, ego is the blindfold that keeps us from seeing ourselves clearly.

What was a time when you were overly invested in a course of action or a specific result—and when you looked at it in hindsight, under the lens of experience, you realized your ego was driving you? What would you do differently if you had the chance to do it over again?

As entrepreneurs, we don't have any choice but to improve. We can't allow our egos to get in the way of what's best for the company and the team. That's why we have to start with developing compassion for ourselves—which is the subject of the next chapter.

2

START WITH YOURSELF

When my brother died, I didn't give myself a lot of compassion. It wasn't even something I thought I needed. I was just in shock, trying to keep going, trying to keep the company afloat.

I never considered mental health or wellness important. To be honest, I thought it was kind of bullshit. There's definitely a mental health stigma in the military and in the business world. So instead of getting help or working on myself, I would work eighty-hour weeks and go home and have a few drinks (or maybe more than a few), and nothing would change.

In some ways, it can feel easier to go through life without self-awareness. It's hard to sit down and take a look at yourself and realize how your behavior is affecting yourself and the people you care about. It's a hard pill to swallow. But the truth is that you can't get better—you can't get to the next level or break through the ceiling of what you're capable of right now—until you know yourself and what you need to change.

That's why in the moments when you're struggling, even the most painful ones, it's so important to sit with them and process. That self-understanding is the start of self-compassion.

I would like to think that if my brother had more self-compassion, he would still be here. But the hard truth about suicide is that you never really learn why. That's something survivors of suicide have to live with. What I can offer you, though, is the chance to learn these lessons for yourself before you're thrown into the deep end and have to learn it the hard way, like I did.

The starting place has to be with you. Entrepreneurs have an impact every day on the people who work with us, but we're also at extremely high risk for suicide ourselves. To help others, we have to help ourselves first. That includes acknowledging our suicide risk and our own mental health challenges and being willing to confront them.

To be compassionate to others, we need to have compassion for ourselves, and we can't have compassion for ourselves until we've taken the time to see, acknowledge, and understand our own reactions and "battle drills" and asked ourselves, "What effect are these patterns really having on the people around me, on myself, and on my business?"

I can say for myself that the answer to this question was not what I expected.

ALL GAS AND NO BRAKES

There's a saying in the military that I referenced in Chapter 1: The best commander that you can have is somebody who's smart and lazy. The worst commander is somebody who's dumb and energetic. The dumb ambitious leader is going to get you into all kinds of trouble and pain, and even worse, you're going to end up doing a lot of it.

When you've got a leader who's smart and lazy, he's going to figure out the best, easiest way to do something, and you're going to be able to do it easily and have time to spend with your family.

For those of you who have never been in the military, let me add some context here. A commander isn't like your boss at work. He decides when you work and when you can go home. He decides whether you go out into the field for three weeks straight and don't see your family, or if you go for one day. Sometimes he even decides what you get to eat. He has a huge impact on your freedom as a soldier.

An entrepreneur doesn't have quite this kind of control over the people who work for you, but you have a lot more impact than you realize. Just like military commanders, entrepreneurs have the ability to make life pretty shitty for a lot of other people with just a few words or a single assignment.

Entrepreneurs aren't the dumb and energetic type; we're usually pretty smart people. But we also tend to be all gas and no brakes. It's like we have to be showing everyone around us, all the time, that we're doing the most work and carrying the heaviest load.

Like anything else that's worth doing, compassion takes energy. It takes effort to learn to be more compassionate in general, and it takes planning and intention to be compassionate on any given day, or with any specific person. If you're packed wall-to-wall, doing work to look like you're the busiest one in the company, or spending all your time in meetings that you don't need to be in, you won't have the time or energy, or frankly the interest, to do the work to become more compassionate.

A lot of leaders will say that they don't have time for compassion because they're busy with the business. That's what I would have said, too. But that's a misperception. Working on compassion is working on the business on a deep level.

Imagine two companies in the same space, going head to head. One has a culture of compassion, where everyone knows each other well and cares deeply and takes care of each other, even when things get hard. The other has a culture where everyone is working overtime, the leader is going in every direction at once and not focused on anything, and nobody cares about each other—they're all just making themselves look good or doing the minimum because they don't care about the company, either.

The company that has a culture of compassion is going to win every time. Remember what Peter Drucker famously said: "Culture eats strategy for breakfast." Strategy matters, but the best strategy in the world, without a culture of compassion, will struggle by comparison. When everyone on a team cares about each other and works well together, the execution of the strategy improves exponentially.

In a compassionate company, the team will also have a lot more fun. You'll get to spend time with people you like, you'll do better in the market, and everyone in the company will be better off.

I've been the entrepreneur working insane hours to prove myself and pushing uphill every day against a culture (a culture I helped create!) where nobody cared and compassion seemed like an irrelevant luxury. I understand. I know why it seems like we have to do things that way. We don't.

Right now, I work a few hours a week, attending the meetings I need to attend and letting other people do the work they can do better than I can. These days, a little of me goes a long way. I used to work ninety hours a week, and about three of them were effective. Now I have one meeting a week with my team. It's the most impactful hour in my business—and most of it involves me listening. I can trust my team to do what's needed because I know them, and I care about them—and they care about me and the company and each other.

THE RIPPLE EFFECT

Compassion is more powerful than time or effort because time and effort have absolute limits, but compassion is exponential and self-generating.

If I'm working eighty hours a week, that's already more than eleven hours a day, seven days a week. I'm already stealing from myself and my family to work that much. If I'm putting in what feels like the absolute maximum effort all the time, there's no way to give more, and eventually, even that's going to burn out.

Compassion doesn't work that way. When I act compassionately toward someone, I generate more goodwill and more trust. I feel more curious and open to that person, which generates even more goodwill and trust. And as I approach them with that trust and curiosity, they feel more loyal to me and my company and care more about its success. And it doesn't stop there. My compassion toward them makes them more likely to be compassionate to others.

Even a minimal effort on my end creates ripples that spread out wider and wider, with greater trust and engagement and care and loyalty spreading outward across the entire company. It becomes a self-generating cycle.

That cycle starts with self-awareness.

The more self-awareness we have as entrepreneurs, the more we see and understand the impact we're having on ourselves and others. That leads to being able to see both our strengths and our weaknesses, and to lean into our strengths and improve in the areas we're not as strong in.

The result of that self-awareness work is self-respect, although that can seem paradoxical at first. Before I started my reflections and meditation and self-awareness journey, I often struggled with insecurity. I was a young commander in a platoon with older, more experienced soldiers. Then I took over a construction company with no experience in construction, again leading a team that had more years of combined experience than I would ever be able to catch up to.

You might think that stepping back and reflecting on your own behavior would make you feel worse. But actually, I started to see where I add incredible value to my organization and what work I should actually be doing. Allowing myself to objectively reflect on my own behavior, and my own strengths and weaknesses, let me see that of course I would never be the most experienced person in the company for technical construction questions, and I would never be the best project manager. But I didn't want to be a project manager, and I didn't need to be a technical expert. I needed to be a leader.

Those insights made me more able to step back from my ego and have more curiosity about the people and the environment around me, to see where I added value, where they added value, and what work each of us should be focused on. It also gave me a chance to learn from others in a way that grew my own expertise.

I'll give you an example. When I first started coaching entrepreneurs, if I walked into a coaching session and saw an older, experienced leader in the room, I would act more aggressive and more assertive in order to assert that I was in charge and that I knew things. I was constantly proving that I was the right choice and that I deserved to be the one running the show. In reality, I was intimidated because I didn't understand compassion. Unfortunately, it was often perceived as me not liking him, which didn't make the coaching easier.

As I started to do my self-awareness work, I saw this pattern, and I asked myself, "Why am I doing this?" Basically, I was afraid. I was afraid he'd make me look bad in front of the other people in the room by questioning my expertise or disagreeing with me. I was afraid, fundamentally, that I didn't belong in the front of the room.

Becoming aware of that pattern let me step back and think about what was really happening. I realized that there was another way to see it. This experienced leader had come to me for coaching. That wasn't questioning my expertise—it validated it.

This revelation totally changed my perception of the experienced people in my sessions. Now, I welcome the breadth of experience these people bring, and it becomes an amazing resource for all of us to draw on. There's a saying in sales that it's best to have happy clients who can help you, and share their experiences with prospects, because that's more authentic and meaningful. Coaching is similar in that it's helpful to have someone in the room with experience that I can draw on to help the rest of the team with whatever exercise we're working on.

That first step in self-awareness, simply recognizing that I was reacting aggressively to this particular kind of client, led me to see something in myself that I hadn't noticed before, and I became a lot more open and curious. Instead of immediately gearing up for a fight, I let myself listen to what these older clients had to say. Sometimes I learned something from them, and because I wasn't obsessing about my own fears, I was able to incorporate their knowledge into the coaching session.

Despite my fears, nobody started going to him for coaching because he said something intelligent. Instead, it made me look like a real leader. It led to *more* respect, not less.

Plus, I could have more compassion and understanding for the clients I hadn't clicked with before. I could understand that maybe the aggressive person in the room was feeling the same thing I was feeling: fear that he wasn't good enough or that he would be challenged in front of his peers. And instead of making it worse by justifying his fears, I could be compassionate and curious, and create an environment where we all brought our knowledge together. We all learned more, and the coaching sessions went better.

It's what's called a virtuous cycle, where putting even a little effort into something creates more of it, which then comes back to you exponentially and keeps the cycle going. The compassion spiral looks like this:

When I started running the business, I was doing the opposite. It's a lower level of consciousness, a survival-based mindset. And unfortunately, like a virtuous cycle, it tends to create more and more of itself—only in the other direction.

When you're in a survival mindset, you don't have the time, energy, or interest to invest in self-awareness. Your curiosity about others is limited, and you close yourself off or focus on what you look like or how other people see you, instead of trying to see them. You're less aware of others and what they need, and you become pushy, telling people what to do instead of letting them be experts in their own work.

I know that when I'm in that mindset, that's when I get overly salesy and try to force the outcome I want. It's like I'm constantly thinking, *I need to get my needs met!* and assuming they won't be. It's a very *me, me, me* attitude.

Intent matters, too—even behaviors that look like compassion can be self-centered if they're done for selfish reasons. Acting like you care about someone to get what you want isn't altruistic, and it will be obvious.

It might sound counterintuitive, but when you care genuinely about the other person, they will care about you, and then they will *want* to help get your needs met. One of the oldest concepts on Earth is the idea of karma: that you get back what you give. That's how compassion works, too. And like karma, the way to kick-start the cycle of abundance is to become aware of your own actions and their consequences.

NEGATIVE SELF-TALK

The clearest sign that you aren't practicing compassion for yourself is negative self-talk.

You can tell when someone does negative self-talk because you can hear it in the way they talk about themselves to other people. They'll say, "Ugh, I really messed up in that meeting" or "I can't believe how stupid that was."

Then the other person walks away thinking, "This guy is so hard on himself, I wonder what he's saying about *me*." Often, they'll assume that being critical of yourself means you're also critical of everyone else. Whatever you say about yourself, they hear it as if you're talking about them.

Negative self-talk is ultimately based on perfectionism, the idea that we should do everything right at every moment of the day and with every person in our lives, without error. This kind of perfectionism can seem like a way to push ourselves, to make sure we're doing the best we can, but in fact it doesn't work that way.

Perfectionism is toxic. It gets you so focused on reliving past mistakes or obsessively trying to avoid future mistakes that you become totally blind to your own successes, to the people around you, and to the opportunities that are coming up. If you can't forgive your own past mistakes, you won't forgive others, either, and your company can develop a culture of cover-your-ass and blaming, or become so risk-averse that real growth isn't possible.

The antidote to negative self-talk is visualization. It performs a similar function in helping to prevent mistakes, but it focuses on how to make success happen rather than assuming you'll mess up.

I first learned visualization in the Army. We took a course on Warfighter Performance Psychology, where we learned to visualize success and trained our minds to be more successful. Part of it was seeing in our minds, in detail, every aspect of a mission. We would walk through every single step in a mission, visualizing our own part and thinking through everything that could possibly happen.

That's not the same as perfectionism because instead of self-judgments and blame, it focuses on solutions and plans.

After the Army, I was a high school wrestling coach, and I took the visualization practice with me. We would walk the kids through every single thing that would happen in the match: what the gym would look and feel like, how they'd approach the mat, what they would do if an opponent made this move or that move. And it worked. Visualization and true self-awareness began to replace beating themselves up, even after a loss.

You can do the same thing as an entrepreneur.

When I realized my pattern of becoming defensive in coaching meetings, I started using visualization to make better choices. I would visualize in detail the coaching room or the Zoom call. I would imagine an older, very experienced leader in the room, and notice my feelings of inadequacy or the thought that *I don't deserve to be coaching this person.* Then I would intentionally visualize switching my approach. I imagined asking him questions, welcoming his advice, bringing him in instead of trying to shut him out. I visualized everything that might happen as a result. Yes, he could try to take over the meeting. But he could also become a valuable partner.

Over time, I was able to start responding the way I wanted to—and the result was that people respected me more, not less.

It is the opposite of self-compassion to hold yourself to an unattainable standard.

Self-awareness is the solution because instead of berating yourself, you start to ask *why*. "Why am I so laser-focused on this one outcome? Why am I so reactive in this situation?" The answers to these kinds of questions help you figure out what you really need and open up new ways to get there, rather than being obsessive about one particular result.

That's the switch from negative self-talk to curiosity—and curiosity is at the heart of compassion.

COMPASSION IS CURIOSITY

A few years ago, I hired a new leader in the company. I was hyper-focused on growth, and he talked an amazing game about how he was going to bring in new clients and exponentially grow our revenue.

It didn't take long to realize he was not a good fit.

The first thing that tipped me off that he didn't really care was that he showed zero curiosity. In retrospect, something he said in his interview should have been a huge red flag, although I wasn't mature enough to recognize it at the time. When I asked him, "What aren't you good at, and what don't you like doing in the business?" he responded with, "I love everything." A person who says they love everything either hasn't developed enough self-awareness to understand what they don't like, or they're hiding something. The question is designed to understand where a prospective candidate will focus their time, not to trick them or pressure them to be good at everything. I can see now that I had the tools, but I didn't know how to use them.

I knew what questions I should ask, but I didn't pay enough attention to what a good or bad answer would look like because I was so focused on growing the business.

Everything he did while he worked for us was a red flag. He didn't want to learn about other people or their ideas. He didn't ask, "What would you do in this situation?" His whole attitude was *do what I tell you to do, get out of my way, and don't make me look bad.* He was very clearly out for himself, and people could see it right away.

The final straw was when a member of my team, someone I really trust, told me, "If this guy is still here next year, I won't be—not because I'll leave, but because he'll fire me to bring in his own people that will be loyal to him above all else." He was building his own fiefdom.

I decided I had to let him go. I sat down with him and said, "You know, when I was in the military, something I learned the hard way was that you have to show people you care about them first, before you ask them to do things for you." He said, "I do that! When so-and-so had COVID-19, I sent them a card."

At that point, I knew for sure he had to go. He didn't even have the self-awareness to know what caring about people looks like. We already had a culture of caring about each other that started when my dad was in charge, and he didn't even see the point.

A good leader should be like a good coach. Your job is asking the right questions and getting curious, finding out what the other person knows and thinks and cares about and wants. That's not the same, by the way, as saying, "Have you thought about doing X?" That's advice pretending to be a question, and advice is the opposite of compassion. It assumes that I know better than you do and basically treats you like an extension of me and my ideas, rather than your own person. When you immediately leap to giving advice instead of asking questions, that's a good sign you're not self-aware or curious.

The self-aware person, and even the person who is just trying to become more self-aware, starts with curiosity. In particular, they step back from outcomes and look at causes. If a meeting felt like it was all conflict and no solutions, why did that happen? If a person in the company isn't performing at the level they need to be, what might be going on that's causing that?

Over time, this kind of curiosity creates more self-awareness because we start to notice how we as leaders might, sometimes, be the cause of the problem. It's a slow process, first noticing that the same thing keeps happening, then starting to see our own part in it.

ALWAYS STILL LEARNING

I want to make it clear that I'm not perfect at any of this. I'm still learning and practicing, and I still mess up all the time. This is a journey—but it can't start until we're aware that we want to improve.

There's a concept in psychology called the Dunning–Kruger effect. Basically, it says that the people with the lowest level of competence are the most likely to overstate their competence. When we're bad at something, we don't even know how bad we are, whereas when we know a lot, paradoxically, we're also much more aware of what we don't know.

All of us start at that low point in the Dunning–Kruger curve. Until you start reflecting and becoming aware of your own patterns, it's not possible to know how they're affecting people. You don't know what you don't know.

Dunning-Kruger Effect

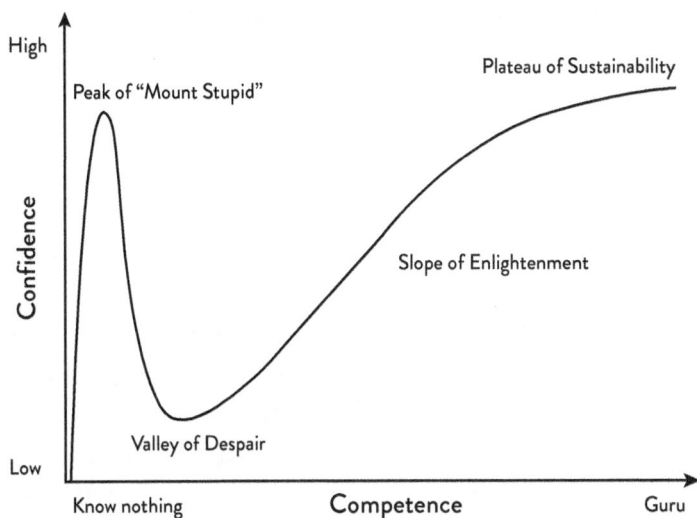

For me, a lack of compassion and curiosity often shows up as interrupting people. I'll be in a meeting, and suddenly I'll look around, and I can tell from the looks on their faces that they're thinking, "He doesn't care what I think." That shuts them down, and instead of getting all the good ideas from my team, I'm telling them what to do and trying to control the outcome.

Before I became aware of my tendency to interrupt, I just barrelled through the meeting. I assumed they weren't saying anything because they didn't have anything to say.

This isn't just a lack of compassion. It's also ineffective leadership. I'm not letting my team make decisions. I'm not hearing all the ideas or all the information that could lead to the best solution. And the reality is, I'm not smarter than they are. They are smarter than I am in their own areas—that's why they're in those seats. When I sit and listen, we get the best answer every time because it's the answer they believe in and will run with.

If you want proof that I'm still learning, I made the same mistake just this morning. I interrupted a member of my team who was explaining something, and he just said, "No, you go ahead." I never got the rest of what he was going to say, and I know that was a loss for me and for the company.

Fortunately for me, and for my company, I've been doing the same exercises I'm coaching you on in this book. Before, I would have had no awareness at all that I'd missed out on what they had to say. Now, because I'm obsessed with my relationships with my team and how well we're working together, I reflected on it and noticed it immediately. I went back to that person, apologized, and asked them to expand on their idea. It's very powerful when a leader apologizes and says, "Hey, that's on me. I messed up." We should be messing up; if we're not making mistakes, we're not trying. Owning those mistakes sends a powerful message.

In that case, not only did the team member know I cared, but they shared an insight that I wouldn't have otherwise gained.

This work, building self-awareness and curiosity and compassion, is a journey. You're not going to become perfectly compassionate overnight. The good news, though, is that every single action you take toward becoming even a little more curious or self-aware or caring will have exponential results.

RELATIONSHIPS ARE SELF-COMPASSION, TOO

A few months before my brother died, he moved back to Seattle. It seemed to me that he struggled with maintaining relationships, especially the closest and least transactional relationships. Speaking from my own relationship with him, it seemed like the closer the relationship, the harder it was for him to maintain it. I can't pretend to know what it was like for him those last few months, but I do know that he worked from home, and it seemed to me that in the end, he had pushed away pretty much everyone and had very limited interaction.

There's a reason solitary confinement is so detrimental to human mental health. We are social animals, and when we're more connected to others and caring for each other, it quenches a basic thirst we have as human beings. The National Alliance on Mental Illness has reported that inmates who have experienced solitary confinement are 78% more likely to die by suicide in their first year after release, compared to inmates who never experienced solitary. They note that solitary confinement exacerbates existing mental illness and can even cause it.

Maintaining positive relationships isn't just about supporting other people. It's good for you, too. I've talked with a lot of older leaders about their careers, and without exception, they all say that looking back, what they most valued with their interactions with other people.

It's not just about how you treat your family or the people who have worked with you for a decade, as important as that is. How we treat the person we interact with for 30 seconds today should be the same as the way we treat the person we've known for 30 years. The way you approach people is powerful: you can make somebody's day or ruin it in a few seconds. If someone can ruin your day in 30 seconds by cutting you off in traffic or being rude to you in public, just imagine as an entrepreneur the enormous impact you have on the lives of the people on your team.

Changing the way you interact with and affect people takes effort. Just surrounding yourself with other people isn't the same as having relationships. People who live in cities can be surrounded by millions of other human beings but not be connected to any of them. The key is setting an intention, literally deciding ahead of time that you will put the relationship, the connection, the curiosity, and the caring ahead of the drive to get to the next thing.

BUILDING THE HABIT OF SELF-COMPASSION

Building habits is important because, whether you know it or not, you already have built-in patterns of behavior and response that you go to all the time, especially under stress. In the Army, we called these "battle drills": the trained-in, go-to responses that tell you how to respond quickly to any situation.

Your body and mind have their own battle drills, built in from a very early age. The more you have on your plate, and the less you're paying attention to your own behavior, the more you fall back onto those behavioral patterns.

You can't get to the next level, you can't build your compassion for others or for yourself, until you sit down and take a look at yourself and understand your own battle drills and the effects they are having on yourself and everyone around you.

Don't get me wrong. This is *hard*. It's a hard pill to swallow to realize that your own behavior might be the problem. When I am in my most stressed-out state, it's still hard for me to stand back and say, "I'm interrupting, I'm not letting these smart people give me the benefit of their expertise." It's hard not to fall into command-and-control mode. But by now I've built enough habits that I'm able to notice when it's happening and re-engage my own practices, whether that's journaling about a tough meeting or talking with my therapist.

The key isn't to just do the same things I do. You need to figure out what works for you and commit to making those behaviors into habits.

The habit of self-compassion has to start with self-care. Self-care is anything you do to make sure you have what you need to be present and caring for others. That can be physical self-care, like working out and eating well, but it should also include mental health and emotional self-care.

When I started running my business, I already had the habit of being in good shape, physically. The habit of working out started in high school with wrestling, then in college with rugby, and then in the Army. When my brother died, and it became so much harder to do even basic things, I was lucky to already have that foundation. It was never hard for me to get to the gym at least a few times a week because that habit was already so ingrained.

In other words, physical health is already such a strong habit for me that I barely need to think about it. I don't need to put any more effort into that. For you, maybe it's where you need to start. Maybe it's just taking a walk once a day or taking a few opportunities during the day to move.

Where I needed to put my effort was on those mental health habits that I had been neglecting. Now I do transcendental meditation and trauma-based therapy. I try to journal every day, or as close as possible. When I do take the time to journal, it completely changes how I approach the day and the results I get.

Part of this mental health self-care is giving myself the grace to do what I can, not the "perfect" version I think I should be doing. With transcendental meditation, for example, they say you should do it twice a day. Honestly, I'm lucky if I get to it a few times a week. And that's fine. That's what works for me. Instead of sacrificing the progress I've made by saying, "It's not perfect unless I do it the full fourteen times a week," I accept that I'm able to do it eight times, and I get a lot of benefit from that.

Once you build good habits, you won't have to work as hard

to keep them going. I'm still in shape even when I take a few days off, and now the same is true with my mental health. I have enough self-awareness that I notice even very small shifts away from how I want to show up, like if I start interrupting more in meetings or being less curious and more directive. That's when I know I haven't been doing my mental health work, and I put myself back on the path without giving myself a hard time.

The time to build these habits is before you need them. I wish I'd built the habits of mental and emotional health before my brother died. It took a tragedy in my life for me to step back, look at my own behavior, and work toward becoming more compassionate. But you can start now, and then when you do need it, self-compassion and self-care will already be second nature.

I hope that no major tragedy happens in your life. I hope you run a successful business and have a happy family life and everything goes well. Although it's important to remember that an entrepreneur can never know everything that's going on in the minds of their team members. Some of them may be struggling and may truly need our compassion just at the moment when we're most distracted or dealing with another problem.

Even if no one around you is struggling, you will still need these habits of self-care and compassion. You'll need them when a critical employee decides to leave the company suddenly, or when you lose a big client, or even when everything is going so well that you get busy and overwhelmed.

The backbone of compassion is self-care, and building these habits will ensure that you can be compassionate, and give yourself grace, even when life gets hard.

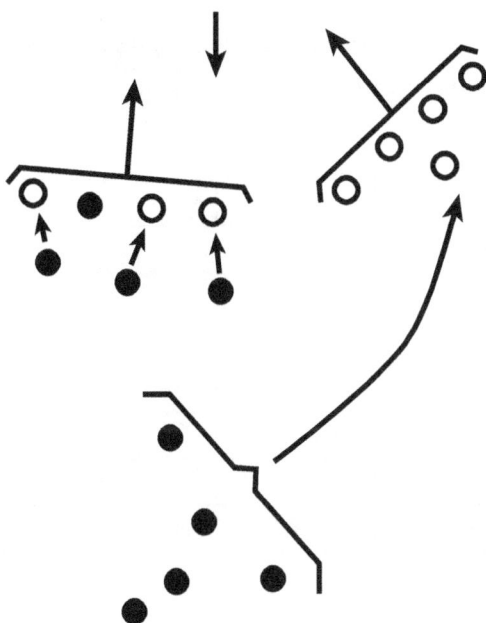

Entrepreneurs tend to be good at tracking and measuring things, so I recommend using a weekly approach to tracking these numbers and starting small. Start with a goal you can actually achieve. If you say you'll journal seven days a week, you're likely to give up the first time you miss a day. Instead, tell yourself you'll do one or two days a month. One day a month of journaling is better than none.

Just like anything else in your business, self-care and self-compassion can be built. Create a plan, measure it, try it out, and adjust based on the outcome. You'll see the benefits, and I bet you'll want to do more. Below is an example of how I track these numbers for myself.

If you need one more reason to do this work, I can tell you this from my own experience: so many people aren't self-aware that if you are, you will stand out immediately. People will respond to it, even if they don't quite know what makes you different.

	GOAL	4/6	4/13	4/20	4/27	5/4
ALCOHOL-FREE DAYS	7		II	I	IIII	JHT II
MEDITATIONS	6		IIII	II	I	JHT I
JOURNALING	7		III	III		JHT II
WALKING MILES	20		JHT	II	III	JHT JHT JHT JHT
RUCKING MILES	5		X			JHT
WORKOUTS	5		X	II	III	JHT
THROW WITH MY SON	3		III	I	III	III

DISCOVERY EXERCISE: LIFE BEYOND THE TO-DO LIST

While I was working on this chapter, my son went over to play with a friend, and his friend's dog bit my son in the face. We had to go to the hospital, and the next day, I kept my son home from school and spent the day with him.

It turned out to be a master class in compassion.

First of all, my son is just such an amazingly compassionate person. The first thing he said, while he was being taken to the hospital with his face mauled up and bleeding, was, "I just hope nothing bad happens to the dog." I assumed he would be most worried about the possible damage to his face, but all he could think about was that the dog wasn't to blame. He knew that when a dog bites someone, the outcome usually isn't great for the dog, and that's what he was worried about. That is a powerful level of compassion. (In case you're wondering—the dog is fine, and the boy's mom now keeps it away from other people.)

The other lesson came the next day when we were at home. He was feeling better than I expected, so I asked him what he wanted to do. He said, "I just want to play video games and watch movies." So I told my leadership team that I wasn't working and spent the day doing whatever he wanted.

There was definitely a time in my life when that would have felt like a waste, or when I would have been anxious and stressed the whole day because of what I was missing at work.

All I could think now was, *Look what I'm getting.* I was spending time with my son. He needed me, and I was able to be there for him. Nothing that I could possibly have accomplished at work, even on the best and most productive day of my career, could ever be that important or that meaningful.

So here's the prompt, in honor of my son:

Write down all the bonus things you got to do because you didn't do the stuff on your list.

As entrepreneurs, most of us have to-do lists that could go on infinitely. There's never a time when there is just nothing we could be doing. When we don't get everything on the list done, we tend to think of that as "waste."

What if you noticed, instead, what you got to do because you didn't get to some item on that never-ending list? Who did you spend time with? What did you do for yourself or your family?

What additional life did you experience because, even for a short time, you acted as a human being, not just a human doing?

3

COMPASSION
IS A MINDSET

In the 1990s, my dad's business almost went bankrupt.

When the business was at its lowest ebb, he took all the money we had left, went to Las Vegas, and bet it all on black. He won. The next day, he came back with his winnings, and it was enough to keep going. It was an act of sheer desperation, and if it hadn't worked, the company I now run wouldn't exist.

For a couple of years, I rarely saw him at all. He was working his tail off, putting everything he had into the company. I remember writing notes to put in his car before he left for work. His stress was so palpable to me, even as a kid, that I was constantly worried about him. I'd write him notes that said, "I love you, dad." I almost never saw him in person, so that was a way for me to communicate with him and show him that I could see how hard he was working.

He used to keep $50,000 in cash in a bag tied up in our

basement because he was so worried about losing it all. Keep in mind, that was the 90s. $50,000 was a lot of money back then. Whether I was consciously aware of it or not, that stress and worry about money colored everything in my childhood.

My dad was doing everything he knew how to do to keep us safe and provide security for our family. My grandfather grew up in the Depression, and he was a WWII POW who escaped from a POW camp not once, but twice. He came back from the war, started a family of nine, and supported us on a shoestring until he built the business. My dad grew up in that culture of scarcity and loss, so it's no surprise that he inherited that mindset around money and scarcity.

Even though I can see how reasonable it seemed to him, his behavior also deeply affected my own relationship with money. It's a big part of why I get so anxious, and push myself so hard, and push other people so hard, when it comes to survival and security.

When it felt like my family's financial security was threatened, or the security of the business, I was no longer able to see the big picture. I'd get distracted by tiny setbacks and become overbearing and pushy. I would have a single bad month and think, "Is the company dying?" I'd get pissed off and angry and go around finding things wrong with everyone in my business—and at home—and giving them my "great advice" on what they should be doing differently.

A lot of entrepreneurs are this way, not just about money but about all kinds of outcomes in the business. We get bad results, or even just less great results, and then we get testy and hard to talk to—right at the moment when we need to be accessible and engaging. Our job in that moment is to lead the team to a solution and help them row the boat.

Therapy helped me see that my reaction to money was a

mindset. It wasn't a mindset I chose necessarily, but one that was handed down to me. We all have these ways of thinking and reacting that were taught to us by our parents or our early experiences, and they can be hard to see because they're so ingrained in our lives. Furthermore, our parents often don't realize they are ingraining these mindsets in us. And here's a shocker: we are probably doing the same thing with our own children. I like to joke that I won't know what I messed up as a parent until my kids are adults. Then we'll see what I did well and where I dropped the ball.

What's powerful about seeing these reactions as mindsets is that your mindset can be changed. I first learned that in Special Operations training. They taught us visualizations to change our mindsets. We would visualize every possible event or scenario that could happen during a mission. It was called "forward thinking." We'd practice each step, thinking through, "Okay, so if this happens, I'll do that," and so on. That way, even when things went wrong, we'd be able to follow the mindsets and habits we had practiced instead of falling back on our stress patterns.

If you want to be more compassionate, more curious, and more self-aware, you need to do the work to intentionally create those new mindsets.

WHY MINDSET MATTERS

It can be hard to pinpoint the exact business value of mindset because it's so internal. The way a person approaches or thinks about things like money, results, setbacks, and relationships isn't measurable. It can't be tracked with KPIs.

Nonetheless, the leader's mindset has more impact on the business than almost anything else he brings to it. Mindset dictates performance.

A mindset is something that we cultivate with an individual, internal effort. It's about changing our own performance by changing how we respond—intentionally rather than instinctively.

On the days that I take the time to visualize how I want to respond and react during the day, everything goes better. I have better interactions. I stay open to new ideas. The team solves problems better because I give them the space and trust to do it. My mindset dictates my own performance, which has a cascade effect on the team.

Because mindset is internal, it's almost impossible to look at someone else and say that they have this or that mindset. It's not about making judgments about other people's mindsets or teaching your team to approach things differently. It's about shifting *your own* mindset as the leader and watching the effect that has on everyone around you.

THE WAR FIGHTER AND THE ENTREPRENEUR

The war fighter and the entrepreneur have a lot in common. They both have a kind of natural drive, a willingness to put the mission or the company objective or the desire to build something over their own comfort. As a result, they tend to also be driven to learn and to gain mastery in a lot of different areas. Truly professional special operators and entrepreneurs are always learning and trying to get better. They understand Marshall Goldsmith's insight that "what got you here won't get you there," and they're always trying to get to the next level by upgrading their skills.

Those characteristics will absolutely help you in learning new mindsets, but that natural drive isn't itself a mindset.

A mindset is something you're intentional about, something

you cultivate on purpose because it serves you and those around you. So while we as entrepreneurs do tend to have an innate ability to go out and create value and drive our businesses forward, we still need to add on deliberate mindsets.

One of the most important mindset shifts for me has been balancing accomplishments and success with gratitude. I haven't given up the drive to do better, be better, and accomplish more, but I've tempered it. Gratitude doesn't have to mean "I'm happy with what I have, and I never want more." I've learned that I can be deeply grateful for everything I have in my life—especially my relationships and the people around me—and simultaneously honor the drive to success that has gotten me where I am.

For me, that balance is the ultimate form of freedom. Success at the expense of freedom isn't actually success; it's failure. An entrepreneur who is monetarily rich but works every weekend is not wealthy. He's poor in a way that's going to affect his long-term ability to succeed and probably damage his health, too.

What exact mindsets you cultivate for yourself will depend on the self-awareness we talked about in Chapter 2. You have to figure out, for yourself, what matters to you. What's most important in your life? As I became more self-aware, I realized that what matters most to me is my family, having a good life, having good relationships with my team, and being compassionate. The monetary rewards became the byproduct of those healthy, productive relationships and behaviors.

Understanding that led me to a few specific mindsets that drive my compassionate approach to leadership.

THE FOUR CORE MINDSETS OF
COMPASSIONATE LEADERSHIP

The mindsets that lead to compassion are trust, abundance, curiosity, and empathy.

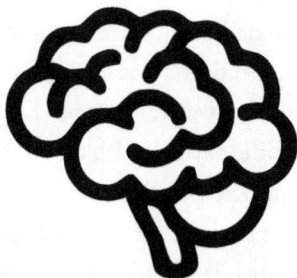

Each of these also has an opposite mindset that diminishes compassion. Cultivating them means intentionally taking action toward the compassionate mindsets—and also being self-aware enough, and self-compassionate enough, to notice when you're moving in the other direction, forgive yourself for mistakes, and keep working on it.

TRUST VERSUS DISTRUST

DISTRUST ⟷ TRUST

Trusting people isn't about not verifying, and it doesn't mean giving up oversight or even micromanagement, when it's necessary. As one leader during my Army days put it, "If something is really important, I will micromanage it."

As a mindset, trust is an intention to allow the experts on

your team to be experts and to do the jobs you've hired them to do. It means deciding to ask good questions and wait for the answers instead of immediately telling people what to do or how to do it.

With trust, I'm able to show compassion to the team by letting them get on with their jobs and treating them like competent professionals. It's also compassionate to myself because it means I no longer work ninety-hour weeks. After all, the more you give instructions, the more people will come to you for instructions, and the more instructions you'll have to give. That creates dependence, and it's also exhausting.

The key to actively cultivating trust is figuring out what you can let the team do on their own, and where your presence is needed. It's a continuous process, not a one-time decision. Just because we make progress doesn't mean we stop. We keep going to the gym to stay fit. Our companies are always trying to add more value for clients and be better places to work. We're always getting better at relationships.

Once, at the gym, I was asked, "Why are you working so hard? What are you training for?" My answer was that I'm training for fucking life, because life is hard. We're never done with this work. Fortunately, we can see progress along the way, and that keeps us coming back.

IS THIS A LEAF ISSUE OR A TRUNK ISSUE?

YOUR BUSINESS

I carry a bookmark with me that has an image of a tree on it. It's a reminder to be constantly asking myself whether I need to be involved in a particular problem or issue, or whether I can let my team handle it.

If your business is a tree, and something happens to the leaves, that's normal. Leaves fall and grow back all that time. The tree's not going to die because it loses a leaf. If something happens to the trunk or the roots, that is a problem. That's when you as the leader need to be involved.

I'm not saying I made this up. A lot has been written using the analogy of a tree for business. People have talked about the health of the leaves being a reflection of the health of the roots, or about how to grow your tree more sustainably. For me, the tree analogy is most useful as a way to think about where I should put my energy.

In meetings, I'll keep the bookmark in front of me and ask the team, "Are we talking about a leaf here, or the roots?" If we're talking about leaves, I shut my mouth. That's a great time to underwrite the team learning something and building independence. If we're talking about the roots or the trunk, that's when I start to ask questions.

This practice gets me out of a lot of decisions I don't need to be involved in and frees me up to do the work that only I can do. But it does a lot more than that. I can use the leaf issues to elevate the team, to invest in their learning. Those are opportunities for them to demonstrate their abilities and for me to learn about them as people.

That tree bookmark is a perfect example of the intentional cultivation of a mindset. It represents my commitment to developing trust in my team and my investment in them as people. I'm treating them as capable human beings and showing that I care about their growth, and that's the cornerstone of compassion. The bookmark is a physical reminder of that commitment that helps me stick to it.

ABUNDANCE VERSUS SCARCITY

SCARCITY ←———————→ **ABUNDANCE**

A lot of people have written about the scarcity mindset and the abundance mindset, but it's important enough to talk about here. An abundance mindset is the belief that there is, and will be, enough—enough time, enough money, enough opportunities, enough clients.

It's not about the accumulation of wealth; it's about there being *enough*. It's not a greed thing—it's a peace thing. It's not about constantly growing revenues, but about the idea that if we do our work well, we will get what we need. A scarcity mindset is the feeling that there is never enough, or that life is a "zero sum" game that requires competing over every resource.

For example, a scarcity mindset frantically tries to sell to every single potential client without thinking about whether the client is a good fit or what the job will entail. Scarcity feels like "no amount is ever enough," so there always needs to be more, no matter what its quality.

An abundance mindset understands that you might need to let one client go so you can cultivate the clients you want. I've had clients in the construction business who wouldn't trust my team to do what they are experts at. They questioned every move and refused to give us the trust to do the work. That's not about money—it's about a mismatch of values.

But we tend to act from desperation, from the feeling that we have to land this project or we might not ever get another one. That's the scarcity mindset.

Abundance and trust work together closely. When I'm not trusting my team, it's often because I'm in a scarcity mindset. I'm worried that if I'm not involved in everything, there won't be enough clients or revenue, or that people won't see my value because I'm not visible all the time. In fact, the opposite is true. Trusting them to deal with the everyday stuff creates the abundance of time I need to do the work that only I can do and to tackle the "root" issues.

Because of how I grew up, and my dad's and my relationship with money (and probably his dad's, and his dad's...and so on), abundance can be especially hard for me. I cultivate it intentionally by focusing on what "enough" means and by reminding myself of the great clients I gained when I didn't take on the ones I didn't want, or the revenue my team brought in when I stepped back and let them work.

CURIOSITY VERSUS ARROGANCE

Curiosity is the basis of compassion, and the opposite of arrogance. It means asking questions and being open to the answers you get, even if they aren't what you expected. Presumption is going into a situation thinking you already know the best way or the right answer. That kind of arrogance is the opposite of curiosity, and also the opposite of compassion.

I can tell when I'm getting away from curiosity when I hear myself starting to give advice or tell people what to do. When I go into a session with a client or a meeting with a direct report, with an assumption, that assumption is rarely, if ever, correct. When I go in with a curious mindset, we get to a better solution because we use *both* our knowledge and expertise and insight, not just mine.

The worst part is that when I go in and jam something down somebody's throat, I sometimes find out that the idea I was pushing so hard wasn't even right, or wasn't completely right, which means we could be taking a less effective approach all that time until I figure it out. And then I either have to stick to it or go back to the person and admit I was wrong.

Going in with assumptions instead of curiosity has also kept me from growing the business in new ways. When you're curious, you look around at your environment and wonder what else might be possible. When I've been most presumptuous, I wasn't even curious about what the business could be like, what all the different potential growth areas or opportunities might be. I was just focused on one, often limited, outcome I expected to see.

I assumed nothing could change because I didn't see any options. I just kept thinking, *I guess this is my life now. I hope someday it's fewer hours.* I wanted things to be different, but I didn't see how to get there. I felt like I was helpless because

I "had to" be on top of everything in the business. Without curiosity, I couldn't see any other way.

This is absolutely connected to trust and abundance issues because having everybody report to one leader, creating that dependence, forces that one person to have, or seem to have, all the answers. If everybody is coming to me for every decision, I end up advising them on every little detail, even in areas where they know a lot more than I do.

This isn't just a question of ethics or generosity, either. It's a hard, practical reality. It's well known that you can't scale "tell." If you have to answer every single question or make every decision, there's an absolute cap on how big your business can get, based on the number of hours in your week.

When I approach my team with curiosity instead, all of us are able to see how much each other knows—and that builds my ability to trust them and my sense that there is an abundance of expertise and competence. That abundance lets the business grow beyond what I can personally control. It's a self-reinforcing cycle.

Now, I make myself sit back and listen, or even remove myself altogether. I used to be in meetings all week long, giving out advice and feeling like nothing could get done without me. Now I'm generally in about one meeting a week, and that's with my senior leadership.

This isn't just a nice theory. It works. The other day, I was invited to the weekly Operations Department meeting at my company. I've been walking by this meeting for years, wondering what they were up to in there. I've held back my desire to get involved, but still, I would always walk by and think, *Are they missing important stuff? Are they doing what I would do?*

So when I was invited to the meeting to share an EOS® concept, I was secretly thrilled. Now I could find out what they were up to. I ended up sitting through the whole meeting without saying a word until my presentation. They were crushing it. They did not need me. Even better, the meeting itself was a model of curiosity and collaboration. It wasn't one person barking orders or an endless series of slides. They worked through small issues quickly, sat with the big questions until they were solved, and did it all in less than the allotted hour, including the time they gave me to present.

Old me, the version of myself who had to prove my importance at every turn because I was insecure about my own value to the company, would have been threatened by the fact that they clearly do not need my help. My work on self-awareness has turned that around 180 degrees. Not only did I tell them what a great job they were doing, but I was relieved and happy to find out that I wasn't needed.

I've got all that time and energy back, I don't have to worry about what they're doing, and I can focus on the work that only I can do.

Curiosity is compassionate because it sees my team as human beings, professionals, and experts, not as tools or extensions of my own agenda. It's compassionate because these human beings spend a huge amount of time at work, and when I treat them with curiosity and trust, the hours they spend at work feel meaningful. They go home feeling competent and effective instead of resentful or devalued.

It's also compassionate to me because I no longer work punishing hours or spend all my time worrying or angry that people aren't doing things the way I would do them. And that helps me develop the last compassion mindset, and maybe the most important: empathy.

SELFISHNESS ◄————————————► EMPATHY

Being an entrepreneur can sometimes feel like being a lone wolf. We tend to be high on initiative and focused on achieving our own goals. That kind of drive can sometimes push us to become selfish. I don't mean selfish in the sense of keeping everything for ourselves or not being generous. I mean selfish in terms of self-focused: seeing only our own goals, noticing only our own achievements, and believing only in our own competence.

Shifting to an empathy mindset means shifting from an individual focus to a team focus. The individual mindset thinks, *What do I want? What do I need to get done?* Empathy asks, *What do we need? What makes everyone happier and more effective?*

Business Is a Team Sport

When Special Operations is evaluating new recruits, they're looking for top performers. Like entrepreneurs, the people who apply to be in Special Ops tend to be driven individuals with a lot of skills and a competitive approach to the world. Those characteristics are necessary to be successful in Special Ops— but they aren't enough.

The military's evaluation of top performers is a graph with two axes. The first axis is performance, the way we're generally taught to think about it: all the individual skills and abilities the person brings with them. The second axis is called "team player." It evaluates how well the individual helps other people be successful.

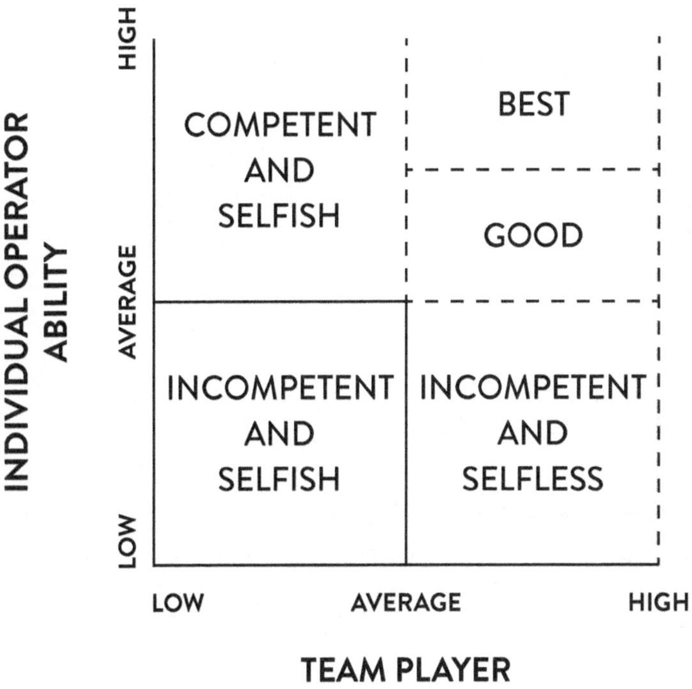
INDIVIDUAL OPERATOR ABILITY
HIGH
AVERAGE
LOW
COMPETENT AND SELFISH
BEST
GOOD
INCOMPETENT AND SELFISH
INCOMPETENT AND SELFLESS
LOW
AVERAGE
HIGH
TEAM PLAYER

No matter how amazing or impressive a recruit is on the skill axis, if they aren't high on the "team player" side, they're not a fit. The reason is simple: teams achieve more than individuals.

They also use a powerful method for pushing these young recruits to develop their team mentality. As a Junior Lieutenant in the infantry, you're in your 20s, barely out of college in a lot of cases, and right away they give you a thirty-eight-man platoon. You're one of the youngest people in that platoon, and you're in charge of it.

No one in that platoon is going to follow an authoritarian 20-year-old officer. The only way to succeed is to have a team mentality, to collaborate and respect the expertise of the people around you.

Like the military, business is a team sport, not an individual effort. Paradoxical as it might sometimes seem, the only way to achieve your individual goals is to build up the team and help them achieve theirs.

Empathy is the mindset that makes teamwork possible. Empathy builds on trust and curiosity and allows you to see other human beings as similar to yourself—equally intelligent and equally important.

SHIFTING YOUR MINDSETS

At a basic level, empathy is the ability to feel and understand what others are experiencing. That means understanding what the individuals on your team want to achieve and seeing those goals as equal to your own. It means recognizing that humans have a lot going on in life other than work. They have families and financial needs and illnesses. Being empathetic means seeing those human needs as just as important as your entrepreneurial needs for success or revenue or growth—maybe even more important.

I got a powerful lesson in empathy as the assistant coach of my son's flag football team. We had a really tough game, and the refs weren't helping. They were making a lot of questionable calls. As the game progressed, the head coach started focusing his attention more and more on the refs and getting more and more frustrated. The more he did that, the more I could see the kids' morale start to slide.

My perspective, as a results-driven entrepreneur, was to just want to focus on doing our best. I tried to motivate the kids during the game, and then at the end of the game, I had a discussion with the head coach. For the life of me, I could not understand why he was so focused on the refs, no matter how good or bad their calls. I asked him, "Do you think that life is going to be fair for these boys?" And he said, "No, I don't, but there's no way we can accept these refs making calls like this."

I couldn't get him to change his focus, but that's because I wasn't approaching him with the attempt to understand first. I was approaching him with what I thought was the right answer in mind and needing him to get on the same page with me. After talking with my wife about it and thinking it over, I realized something I'd missed: for him, it wasn't about winning the game, regardless of the refs. It was about justice and teaching the kids to stand up for themselves.

As a Black man, he saw that seeing and calling out injustice was key for the boys and their success. He wanted them to understand that they should always stand up for themselves and stand against injustice, and he was actively modeling that behavior. I failed to see that perspective because for me, it's always about results. I haven't experienced much injustice in my life. Good or bad, I think I've gotten pretty much what I deserved in life. I didn't take the time to understand his point of view, or why he was coming from that perspective, before telling him what I thought we should be doing.

The key to shifting your mindsets is to realize that the ones that got you where you are won't get you to the next level.

As humans, we are always hitting ceilings. These are moments when suddenly, whatever we've been doing isn't working anymore. That is a sign that it's time to change. But change is hard. Special Ops understand how hard it is, and how old frameworks and patterns need to be left behind before new ones can be built. That's why they break you down first before they build you back up. They're pushing the young recruits to drop the entitlement mindsets they tend to bring with them, the sense that they're owed something or that things should be easy for them.

When I was growing up, the mindset I was taught by everyone around me, from my parents to my teachers and coaches, was that results are what matter, and you persevere and keep going no matter what. Seeing situations from the justice mindset, like my son's head football coach did, just wasn't something I ever thought about.

I remember one wrestling match in high school, when I was up against a nationally ranked wrestler. Right after the whistle at the start of the match, he immediately tried to throw me, but I sank my hips, got control, and landed on top of him just before he went out of bounds. In wrestling, there are three positions: top, bottom, and neutral. The wrestlers start off in neutral at the beginning of every match, and when someone gets a takedown (getting their opponent down onto the mat), then they move into the top position.

After my opponent threw me and I got control, we both knew that I had scored two points for a takedown. That made the score 2–0, so he went to the middle of the mat and took the bottom position. I was about to get on top when the ref said, "Stop! That was his takedown. You're on the bottom." He pointed at me. The ref had awarded the takedown to my opponent, even though both my opponent and I knew that it was my point.

I could have had a long, drawn-out fight with the ref. I could have challenged it. But I didn't. I took the bottom position and got ready to execute my escape. As soon as the ref blew the whistle, I executed a standing switch, gained control, got the reversal, and recovered the points I'd lost. I ended up winning the match. I was so focused on results that I didn't let the injustice of the bad call stop me from winning.

The call wasn't right, but the way I was brought up, you don't complain about things like that. Results are the only measure, so you get up and you fight and you win.

The justice issue never occurred to me. It's easy for me to say, "Just go back in and win," because injustice wasn't part of my daily life. When the head coach on my son's team argued with the ref, I didn't even try to understand his point of view. My own mindset was that life is unfair, and the kids needed to learn to persevere and fight through it to get results. His mindset was different. He thought the kids needed to learn to stand up for themselves in the face of unfair treatment. The truth is, they need both.

He and I had a long conversation, and when I got a chance to understand his perspective, I could see that he cared deeply about the kids. His mindset was just shaped by very different experiences from mine. Once we understood each other's mindsets, we both had the chance to grow, and I've been blown away by how well we're able to work together.

Building compassion as a leader requires us to do the work of breaking down our old mindsets and shifting toward trust, abundance, curiosity, and empathy. The good news is that, just like with self-compassion, shifting your mindset has exponential effects. Even a little work goes a long way.

The first thing to do is just ask yourself what ceilings you are hitting right now. What issues keep happening, and what are your current mindsets around those issues? What new mindsets would you need to be successful? That alone can give you the insight to get started.

Then, as you work to shift your mindsets on a deeper level, here are some concrete actions you can take that will show immediate results:

When you get the feeling of *needing* to jump in and interrupt, take over the discussion, or express your opinion, take a deep breath and wait. If it turns out that you do need to get involved, you can always do that. But even one or two deep breaths often allows space for someone else to step in and handle it, which builds trust and gives you the confidence to take another step back.

Learn to be comfortable with silence. This isn't as easy as it sounds. I often feel the need to fill up silence with words, but I've come to understand that this is detrimental because I'm not giving others the chance to step in. People literally need oxygen to breathe so that they can own the problem and speak up.

It can often require a lot of self-awareness work to understand why we feel the need to fill up every space with words. Whether you're alone or with others, expand the amount of time you're able to cope with silence. You'll be surprised what arrives to fill the space.

Practice visualization. I discussed in the last chapter about learning visualization in Special Ops training, specifically thinking through, "How am I going to behave when this or that happens?" I use visualization all the time. If I have a big meeting, I visualize going in with a curious mindset. I type up questions I want to ask, to remind myself to start with questions instead of assumptions. I think through and picture in my mind what I'll do if the meeting is going well, and what I'll do if it's not going well.

Journaling is a powerful tool for visualization. I'll write down, "Let me be curious" or "let me show up with empathy." I'm constantly amazed by what a difference it makes in my entire day to do this kind of visualization in the morning, even if it's just a few minutes.

Finally, start noticing your question-versus-statement ratio. If you're making more statements than questions, start to shift that ratio. In the Army, my medic was doing training on how to react to enemy contact once we started taking casualties. He said that the first step is always to return fire. Intuitively, humans want to help each other, but doing so causes more risk of additional casualties, so the first step is to return fire.

Then he asked us, "What's the first step to medical care on the battlefield?" We guessed that we should find cover, or stop the bleeding, or call in help. The medic shook his head. "No, the first step is to *shut the fuck up*. Yelling and screaming is just going to draw more enemy fire." It's a harsh lesson, but it saves lives.

I've always remembered that, and I use it to remind myself to focus on questions. I tell myself, "Ask a question, and then *shut the fuck up*." It's not how I would talk to anyone else, but it helps me keep quiet and listen instead of interrupting or filling the silence.

No matter what approach you use, though, there's one thing you have to do: you have to mean it. Compassion isn't just a strategy or a tactic for getting what you want. You can't fake it.

DISCOVERY EXERCISE: DAILY MINDSET PREPARATION

For a lot of my life, I lived and worked from a scarcity mindset. I spent a lot of time thinking about what I didn't have, what I might lose, and whether I was capable enough to get what I needed for myself and my family. That scarcity mindset came out in the way I was treating other people, too. I was more reactive and much more likely to tell people what to do than to ask about them or trust their intelligence.

One of my most powerful tools for switching that mindset has been my daily journal. If I'm being honest, I don't get to do it every single day, but I try. And I can tell the difference. On the days I don't do it, I can see myself slipping back into old habits. It's one of the fastest ways to build self-awareness.

After a lot of study of other people's journal exercises and mindfulness prompts, and through trial and error with what worked for me, I came up with my own daily journal exercise. Feel free to use mine, or make up your own.

Use this as a starting point to develop your own daily journaling habit. Even five or ten minutes every morning can radically shift how you show up throughout the day.

I made up the acronym BCLISTSW for my daily journal, and it includes every element of my mindset:

Bonus: This builds on the exercise I mentioned in the previous chapter. I note one or two things I got to do, or have, in my life because I *didn't* do everything on my to-do list. It's a reminder to myself that I'm a human being, not just a human doing. We focus so much on the things we didn't get done, and my "bonus" notes remind me to take the time to pet the dog, go for a walk, spend time with my family—the stuff that's not on my to-do lists.

Conscious Stream of Thought: The very best in the world are able to coach themselves. This stream-of-consciousness exercise is a chance for me to ask myself, "What's holding me back?" I write without editing or censoring myself, and then I review what I've written and pinpoint areas to work on. In particular, I ask myself these self-coaching questions when I'm going through tough times and when I have a hard problem to solve.

Learning: I make an active effort, not only to learn continuously, but to keep track of my learning activities. I ask myself: "What did I do yesterday, or this week, to learn something new? What have I learned about the business or about myself?" Learning is critical for entrepreneurs, and you can't be compassionate unless you realize you are also in learning mode.

Intention: When we don't act with intention, we tend to fall back into old patterns. To counteract that, I set an intention for the day that often starts with the phrase, "Let me be." It's not an "I am" phrase, like "I am successful." It's a way I want to act—an intention for my own behavior. I might say, "Let me be compassionate," or "let me be curious."

Successes: Those of us with scarcity mindsets often forget what we've accomplished, so I take the time to say, "Wow, I did that!" When they're all written down, my successes way outweigh my failures, but I often can't see that.

Therapy: There are some issues or questions that don't belong, that I'm dealing with for myself or in my personal life. I write these down so I don't forget them, and also to remind myself what belongs in my conversations with colleagues, what belongs in coaching, and what belongs in therapy.

Scorecard: For many, many years I was trying to do too much every day, and as a result, there was no way I could ever feel successful. I just had week after week of not hitting the impossible goals I set for myself. Now I take the time to ask myself what I can realistically accomplish, and more importantly, what are the handful of things I need to do that only I can do—where I truly add value. This practice keeps me focused on what's important, and it also gives me momentum because instead of failing over and over, I see myself accomplishing wins. Step back your expectations enough that you can get a couple of months in a row of winning weeks, and your energy and motivation for the work will grow exponentially.

What do I want to learn: Finally, I list the things I need to learn to get to the next level, to up my game as an entrepreneur, as a human, as a father, or in any other area of my life I'm working on.

Try it now: Set aside 10 quiet minutes, get out your compassion practice notebook, and complete your BCLISTSW, based on the descriptions above.

4

LETTING GO

When you work at a company that's been around for almost half a century, there are a lot of old stories. Some of them are really funny, a lot of them sound crazy—and some of them are very telling about the culture of the company and its evolution. One of those stories in my construction company is a story I've heard a couple of people tell about my dad and one of the superintendents who worked for him.

The story I've heard is that the team came in one day and noticed that one of the superintendents hadn't shown up to the job site. They started asking around, "Hey, where's Bob?" and somebody said, "Oh, Mike fired him."

They were stunned. "Well, I hope you're going to hire somebody else!"

"Yeah, he's working on it."

That was it. Nobody knew what happened or why he was fired. Nobody knew if he was going to be replaced, or who was doing his work now that he was gone. My dad had made the decision on his own.

My dad had 40 years in the construction business. He built the company. When he started, he really did have to be in charge of everything. It was a very flat organization. Everybody was equal, and they all reported directly to him. Whenever there was a decision to be made, he made it.

Like a lot of entrepreneurs who start out that way, he had a hard time switching to a new style as the company grew.

After my dad passed away, I was in full-on panic attack mode. I worked 90-hour weeks. I was no fun to be around at home—when I was home at all, which wasn't much. I had no idea what I was doing, and I focused on all the wrong things. I got sucked into all the minute details of every project instead of focusing on the high level view of the company. I even started drinking more to cope with the stress.

I was doing exactly what my dad had been doing, running the company the way I'd seen him do it—except that I didn't have his level of experience or his knowledge of the industry. And I could see myself heading in the same direction, toward burnout and more stress and a lifetime of 90-hour weeks.

In the end, this style didn't work for me. It wasn't a team. It wasn't "trust but verify" because there was no trust. I felt like I had to have eyes on everything at once, and the entire burden of running the company fell on me.

Maybe you're in the same boat: overworked and exhausted, feeling like your business isn't running the way it should or making the amount of money you think it should make. Of course you're frustrated when it seems that way—and of course you don't have the mental bandwidth to be compassionate because you're trying to do everything and be everything to everyone.

When I found myself in that place, I had to learn that there's a beauty in saying "no" to things that weren't a good fit for me and in delegating the work that was sucking my energy away from the core business. I had to find a way to let some of it go.

LEADING FROM BEHIND

In my twenties, I started coaching high school wrestling. I'd wrestled in high school, but I'd never coached before. It was a strange feeling for me because as the assistant coach, I wasn't in charge. I was a leader in the US Army, and I was used to being the one to call all the shots.

The team was in disarray. We were dead last in the conference. When we took over, we only had six athletes on the team, out of the fourteen total we were supposed to have.

My good friend Jeremy (the head coach) and I were two young, basically novice coaches, up against coaches who had wrestled in college and who had already been coaching for ten years, fifteen years, sometimes more. They had successful programs that generated athletes who went on to wrestle in college.

It was a mess. The idea that we could win was a pipe dream. Even considering that we might go to a championship was laughable.

Jeremy was a high-energy coach, involved in every move and every match, yelling out to the athletes and taking charge of everything on the team himself. He ran the team kind of like my dad ran his company: a full-on effort, with him at the center of it all. The fact that the team was so out of shape made him push even harder. He wanted those kids to win, and he was ready to do whatever it took to get them there.

I have a ton of respect for that attitude and that energy, but I brought another perspective. In my time in the military, I'd learned that you had to let people win for themselves. You had to give them the vision, the plan—and then let them execute it. I was convinced the same approach would work for our team. But first I had to convince Jeremy.

Jeremy and I are still great friends, and we hang out and talk often. A few weeks ago, I asked him what he remembered about our coaching, and specifically about my approach to leadership. Here's what he remembers:

What we did was incredible. We had no clue what we were doing, we were 23 years old. And then two years later, we were winning tournaments. After the first, our season record was 18–3, 20–2, and 24–2. We made the 3rd round of state playoffs, and we were the regional runner-up. By the time we left, we'd been conference champions five times, and some of the kids were going on to place in the state finals.

I still run into other coaches—guys who were coaching for ten years before us and have done another ten since then—and they are still impressed by what we did. They tell me, "We don't know how you guys did what you did. As soon as you left, it all crumbled and went back to how it was before."

It was you—it was your compassion and leadership that inspired me. And the kids were inspired by it, specifically by the trust you put in them.

The thing that sticks out to me was the selfless devotion and the compassion. You weren't getting paid. You were volunteering your time. But you inspired me, and it made a big difference the way you trusted the kids. I was running around like a maniac, screaming and yelling, trying to do it all myself, but you told me that you have to let the kids execute, let them be leaders. Compassion through trust.

I would drive myself crazy. I remember one match we were not supposed to win. I was a nervous wreck, and right before the match started, you grabbed me, and you said, "I'm gonna challenge you to sit the fuck down, stay in that chair, and stay calm through the whole match, and I promise you, we're going to do better because of it."

It was a tough love thing. I remember your exact words to this day. You told me to sit in that chair the whole time, and that it would be better. And we won matches that day that we should not have won. A few of our kids beat state-ranked athletes, at least one huge upset.

I know I didn't stay in the chair the whole time because I have a newspaper clipping with a picture of me standing by the mat, screaming. But I stayed in my chair way more than I would have otherwise. You showed me huge compassion, calmed me down, helped me see the value of letting the guys lead themselves.

And it worked. We started to take that calm leadership to the team, and it spoke volumes to them about how we trusted them. And the results were there. The way you interacted with the kids, with me, with the refs, the parents—it made a huge difference in our performance.

I'm not sharing that story to show how great I am, or because I think I was the reason we won. I know I wasn't. Jeremy was a fantastic coach, and we couldn't have achieved any of this without his amazing leadership. Part of that leadership was his ability to change. A good coach has to know when to pivot and when to evolve, and every year, Jeremy grew into a better and better coach. It was inspiring to watch him evolve from good to great.

What we accomplished as a team over those years was remarkable. But what's more remarkable is how we did it: by giving up control.

The entrepreneurs I've known—and I'm including myself—often find it nearly impossible to "sit in the chair" and trust someone else to do the work. We have a drive, a fuel inside that tells us to go, go, go all the time.

That superpower can also be our weakness. We want to do so much, in so little time, and we unintentionally end up stepping on people, taking away their initiative or their own drive. We have so much energy and drive, not only do we have the drive to get it done, we have the ability and the energy to drive people crazy.

When you're a one- or two-man shop, it's unavoidable because you have to do it all. You have to do everything. You're running every aspect of the business, down to paying the internet bill, ensuring vendors are being paid and payroll is met, collecting deliveries for your clients, even opening the mail. You do it all. Entrepreneurs, especially when they're just starting out, have to deal with so many different moving pieces that it's often all they can do to keep up. In a larger organization, there are people who take care of HR, IT, the finances, and keeping the lights on, but for early-stage entrepreneurs, there's no one else to do it for you.

As we grow, though, we tend to keep that mentality or that pattern, forgetting that now we have people we can trust to lead for us.

And it's work we have to keep doing. I'm actually struggling with it right now in my own business. We have a tendency as entrepreneurs to go back over and over to the "I have to do it all" mindset. It's counterintuitive because the more we focus on the things that we're great at, and give up or delegate everything else, the better the results. But it's hard to let that mindset go.

A couple of weeks ago, I was in a meeting and suddenly realized that everyone was looking at me and asking me what I thought about their ideas and their solutions. I was getting sucked back into the details even though I'm literally writing a book about this! I'm not perfect at this. It takes work, and it takes consistency to apply these methods and shift our mindsets.

I think Richard Branson said it best. He was asked, "What do you have to do to be a billionaire?" He said, "You have to give up all your millionaire habits." It's the well-known wisdom of "what got you here won't get you there."

This is why military commanders focus on having clear Commander's Intent. Commander's Intent is the vision of the leader, and it is absolutely essential for a driven leader, not just so you can get where you want to go, but so that you can communicate it to the team and let them run with it. If the team doesn't know where you're going, they can't help you get there. And if you don't share your vision with your team, their only choice is to come to you with every little question.

It's like the difference between knowing where you're driving and following step-by-step instructions. If you know where you're going, there are lots of ways to get there. One person might take the highway, and somebody else goes on the side roads. As long as they both get there on time, it doesn't matter. Plus, if there's traffic or construction, they can find a way around it because they know where they are headed.

If they only get one direction at a time, they have no way to make decisions. It's like you're telling them where to go, but just saying, "Okay, in half a mile, turn left." Then once they turn left, they have to come back to you and say, "What next?" You're spending all your time giving turn-by-turn directions to people who know how to drive and how to read a map.

Figure out where you want to go, find a way to communicate it clearly, and then sit down in your chair and let them figure out how to get there. The beauty of this is that it will enable you to focus on the next thing—your next big idea. You can start working on collaborations and partnerships. The really interesting stuff. You can brainstorm more and keep your eye on the big picture.

THE OPPOSITE OF FREEDOM

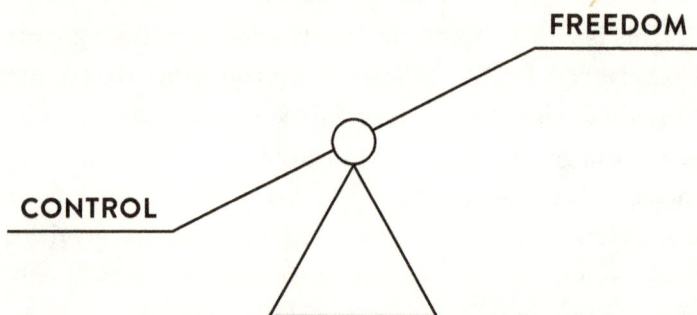

I don't know about you, but I didn't get into running my own business so that I could spend 90 hours a week at work. I became an entrepreneur because I wanted freedom. I wanted the freedom to walk my son to school and to spend time with my family. I wanted the freedom to be myself. I wanted the freedom to do the things I love and that I'm really good at—and the time to focus on them. I didn't want to spend every day doing things that I don't like, that drain my energy and make me not love my life.

I think most entrepreneurs feel this way. We take on the stress and the hard work of running a business because on some level, we want a kind of freedom we can't get in a day-to-day job.

Because of all the work it takes to get the business up to speed and operating, we can get the idea that controlling everything is the path to that freedom, but it isn't. Control is the opposite of freedom.

When you have to control everything, when you're responsible for every decision, you have zero of the freedom that really matters. You're not free to take a day off, enjoy the success of your business, or start new ventures. You're stuck in the daily operations endlessly.

Technologies and management solutions change all the time. The world changes around your business so fast that tomorrow's method could be totally different from today's. But if you lead from genuine compassion and caring, if you share your vision and trust your team to find their own wins, you will be able to shift with whatever changes come up.

I grew up wrestling. As a short, strong guy, I was naturally drawn to it. Now, coaching football for my son, I've realized that coaching football is very different. In football, during the game, the coach is playcalling all the time, and morale management is essential to success. The coach is intimately involved in the management of the game.

In wrestling, you win matches in the mat room during practice, not during the actual match. The reason for this is that the coach can't actually come out onto the mat. Matches are fast, just a couple of minutes, and it's an individual sport. We used to say, "You're only as good as your mat room." As a wrestling coach, all your work is done before the match. Once it starts, all you can do is sit back and watch. You can yell as much as you want, but the wrestler is not going to hear you. Even if he could, it would be almost impossible for him to focus on what you're saying. At that point, it's up to him.

You have to trust him to win on his own.

As entrepreneurs, we need to learn to be more like wrestling coaches. The difference came home to me powerfully the other day in a meeting. We were talking about a land deal, and it was the kind of meeting where, in the past, I would have been trying to manage everything and make all the decisions. I would have tried to be the football coach, calling every play. Instead, I practiced sitting back and letting them figure it out, and they came up with a way to do it that I would never have come up with in a million years.

As I was leaving, I thought about all the expertise in that room. I had a lawyer and an accountant and a real estate expert, and a bunch of other smart and experienced people. There was probably a few hundred years' worth of experience in that room. Letting them speak, and listening to what they say, was a lot easier than me going to law school and learning to be a CPA and getting my real estate license. That would take the rest of my life. I'm never going to get there—and why would I want to, when I have a team of people ready right now?

CONTROL IS AN ILLUSION

One of my best team members came into my office and told me he had some news. He'd decided to leave the company to go work with his son on the beach, building houses together.

I had a choice to make. This is someone I don't want to lose, someone who brings a lot of value to my team. He's going to be hard to replace. And this is a perfect example of me thinking with a scarcity mindset. I'm saying he's going to be hard to replace. I'm going to lose him, and I don't want to lose him.

But if it's going to be better for him—and I'm going to end up finding somebody even better! The old version of myself, the one who wanted to control all the outcomes in my business and worked from a scarcity mindset, would have taken this hard. Even if I was outwardly sympathetic, I would have been pissed off. I would have been thinking, *Great, how do I replace him? What projects is he on? What work am I going to have to do now?*

But that attitude wouldn't have changed anything. That's the hard truth about control. No matter how upset you get, no matter how hard you hold the reins, no matter how you obsess over every detail, in the end, control is an illusion. He was going to leave. No matter how great my company is and how well I treat him or pay him, it's not going to compare with spending the last years of his career on the beach with his son.

Imagine if I had taken the control approach. I could have gotten upset with him and felt hurt and angry, and had tough conversations with him, but they would have been unproductive. I could make all my employees sign non-compete agreements when they start working for me. A lot of companies tie their noncompetes to bonuses, for example, which would mean that if someone had ever gotten a bonus from me, he couldn't work for any other construction company for some period of time after he left mine. He couldn't even work for himself, maybe for years.

What would you get for all that effort and heartburn? If you succeed in convincing him to stay, you've got a team member who doesn't want to be there, who's constantly thinking about how he'd rather be at the beach with his son, and who probably resents his boss for bullying or guilt-tripping him into changing his mind.

That's not good for my company, it's not good for him—and it's not really control, either. It's just the illusion of control.

Eventually, he's either going to leave anyway, or he's going to slack on his work and not be the great employee I wanted to keep in the first place.

I find this happens with clients, too. If I mold and change myself to be what the client wants instead of who I am because I'm trying to control the outcome and land every single client, I end up with clients that aren't a fit for me—and that takes time, effort, and resources from the work I'm meant to be doing.

Instead, my team member came to us as early as possible. He gave us two full months' notice. That's unheard of. He wanted to finish out the projects he was working on and give us time to find somebody else. He cared about us, about the work we're doing, and about not leaving anyone to do his tasks. And it wasn't just about completing the work—he cared about our relationship, too. I still talk to him every couple of months and check in on him.

It was an amazing testament to how deeply the culture of compassion and caring has integrated itself into the company. I was able to pick up the phone and call him and say, "Man, I hate to lose you, but good for you. If you ever need help, don't hesitate to reach out. Running a business is hard, and I'll help any way I can."

It's a testament to him, too, and to the kind of people we can attract into our lives and businesses when we are compassionate. It's not that I'm so great, which makes other people better. It's that when I'm more compassionate, these amazing, thoughtful people want to work with me.

Like all the other practices in this book, I still have to work on this every day. When I wrote the first draft of this chapter, I was irritated because that same day, a meeting had been cancelled. It was an important meeting, in my opinion, and my immediate reaction was to feel frustrated and annoyed. It felt like cancelling this meeting would set back the whole project.

In the grand scheme, a single cancelled meeting is a small thing, but the scarcity mindset tells me there won't be time, the work won't get done. I can imagine a whole cascade of negative outcomes from this one tiny incident.

What happened was the exact opposite. Because the meeting was canceled, I had time to go for a walk. As a result, I was better prepared and in a better mindset for my next business coaching session, and I had terrific rapport with a potential new client.

What's funny, and an even better example of how striving for control is unnecessary, is that now, rereading the chapter again, I don't even remember what that meeting was about. That was just a few weeks ago, and I was so mad, and it didn't matter after all.

The last thing I want to mention here is that control is the default for most entrepreneurs. We tend to default to trying to control things. We're not going to default to freedom because freedom takes a lot of work. Human nature is to try to control things, especially for those of us with this entrepreneurial drive—not to sit back and let things happen. We often don't want to wait and watch and listen and learn.

But when we try to take control, we prevent our teams and ourselves from growing. We grow exponentially when our teams grow, and when we try to control everything, we're just preventing that growth.

SHIFT YOUR METRICS

There are already thousands of books about KPIs, measurement, and keeping track of the things that matter in your business. What I've found is that compassion is the same as any other key indicator for your business: if you don't track it and measure it, it's not going to happen. So what I'm presenting here is how I keep myself accountable to shifting my own mindset.

My goal isn't to be perfect; my goal is to make progress. For example, I keep track of how many times a week I meditate. Sometimes I have really great weeks and hit my goals, meditating as much as I planned. Some weeks I don't. That's okay. I see meditation as key to my life and my business, and therefore I measure it and track my progress.

That required a mindset shift in itself, from seeing meditation and other self-awareness practices as "extra" to seeing them as core practices for my business. One of the practices that has helped me make this shift is having a scorecard. (Using a scorecard is a practice I originally got from EOS®, and I've adopted it into my own leadership with great results.)

We all have ways of keeping track of how we're doing in life, whether it's written on paper or just in our minds, or even unconsciously. For some people, every year on their birthday, they figure out whether they're ahead of where they were last year. Before I started this journey, I didn't have any intentional way of measuring what was important. I was constantly aware of how much money the business was (or wasn't) making, or whether people were doing what I told them, but even that wasn't conscious or focused.

At the end of our lives, what's going to matter is the personal stuff. How much time we spent with our families. How deliberate we were in our actions toward others. What we're attached to and what we've let go of. That's what this scorecard is for.

Think about how you're measuring your own success in life. What outcomes are you focused on? How many of them can you really control? How many of them will you honestly care about at the end of your life—or even next month?

What I've got on my scorecard right now are things like

meditating, having a game of catch with my son, the number of hugs I give my family—all the everyday actions I care about, and that will make me more compassionate.

After all, those are the real reasons I built this business: to support my family, to have the freedom and the time to spend with them, and to care about people. My scorecard helps keep me focused on those outcomes.

Which is why I could say to my former teammate, in all honesty, "Life is short. Go spend time with your son."

CONTROL IS A DANGEROUS DISTRACTION

Control isn't just an illusion—it's also a distraction. Trying to control every little thing that happens in your business ultimately distracts you from focusing on the important work that only you can do.

It's like Jeremy, as a head coach, spending time checking whether everyone on the team had the right lace guards on their shoes, or the CEO of a company who spends weeks or months finding amazing people to be part of his organization and then turning around and micromanaging them and requiring his approval on every single little task.

When Jeremy and I coached together, we assigned team captains and let them do more of the work. At first, we were afraid that high school students might say they didn't want the extra hassle, or they might neglect their duties or mess around. They proved us wrong. Every year, they took more and more on their own shoulders. The logistical work of managing the team just sort of disappeared. We didn't have to deal with any of it. Jeremy, as the head coach, was able to focus on strategy and game plans and supporting the athletes. In other words, he could focus on coaching.

Even better, it was transformational for the kids. They ran with it, and now a lot of them have positions of leadership out in the community, and we can see the effects of what they learned from us empowering them on that team.

Straining for control is also a distraction from compassion. As I've said before, compassion isn't easy or automatic. It takes work and preparation. If you're spending all your time and energy trying to control every tiny outcome in your business, you aren't going to have time or energy to care about people.

The key to letting go of control is self-awareness: figuring out not only what I'm doing, but why I'm doing it.

Am I attending this meeting because they need me, or because I don't trust them to get to the "right" answer? If my team really does need me to attend lots of meetings because they need my input on a lot of issues I don't know much about, that's a different issue. In that case, I might not have the right people on my team. If I have the right people, I can trust them to come to me when they need my insight, and to do the work on their own the rest of the time.

Am I handling all this work myself because I'm the best person to do it, or because I assume no one else will be willing or able? Again, if I have to do the work even though I've hired other people to do it, that's also an indicator that I don't have the right people on my team.

Am I focusing on things I can control—and that only I can do? Or am I holding onto work I shouldn't be doing because I don't trust the people on my team?

Often, in coaching sessions, I ask entrepreneurs to list tasks they could delegate to save themselves time. In one session, an entrepreneur I respect a lot, who runs an incredibly successful business, said, "I want to delegate a certain compliance task that takes me eight hours a week because I don't like it, and I'm not good at it—but I can't."

I asked him, "Do you really want to delegate it then?" He said yes.

So I took a long pause, and he took a long pause, and eventually he said, "It's too important for me to delegate."

In other words, this task was so important that he had to keep doing it poorly. I asked him, "Are you sure it's not too important *not* to delegate?"

We entrepreneurs can be a strange breed. We'll stick to our desire to control and handle everything, even when we can see that it's not serving us. There's a saying, we're going to encounter the same lessons until they're actually learned. Or to put it another way, our pain will continue until we actually shift this mindset.

Just asking yourself questions about what tasks you actually need to be involved in will make a difference—for yourself and for everyone around you. Every time I make even a small move in the right direction in terms of more compassion and less control, I can see it cascade through my whole company and change how everyone is working.

The ultimate freedom isn't when I can give up control to my leadership team. The ultimate freedom is when they give up control to the leaders under them, and those leaders give up control to the people under them, and so on. Giving up control creates freedom throughout the organization for people to be outstanding and do more of the work they're great at. It's the ultimate form of scalability.

LOSING ←————————→ GIVING AWAY

One of the reasons it can be hard to give up control is that most entrepreneurs don't love the idea of "losing." When we talk about control, we often talk about having control versus losing it, and losing control is never a good thing. Losing control is when somebody drinks too much and gets into a fight. In a business context, you lose control when your business is taken over or when outside circumstances make your business model unworkable.

Losing control feels dangerous.

Giving away control is not the same thing. Think about the feeling of giving something away. It can be generous, like giving clothes or food to charity. It can be a relief, like giving away junk that was cluttering up your house.

Giving away control is also easier to accept because you're not saying that no one is taking care of the work—just that someone else is doing it. We didn't lose control of the wrestling team's logistics. We gave that control to the team captains. I didn't lose control of my business's day-to-day finances. I gave away that control to someone who actually knows what they're doing, and who can keep me informed enough to make decisions.

Giving away control doesn't mean giving up on desired outcomes. It means having the trust to let someone else use their own expertise and intellect to figure out how to get there. The result will be not less, but more: more time, more focus, better relationships, and, in my experience, better profitability as well.

When my brother died, I basically stopped working for

three or four months. There's no way I could have stepped away for that long if I'd had a death grip on everything in the business. I had a great leadership team in place, and the business actually grew while I was away. When I got back and saw that, I realized I could step back even more. When we insist on having control over every little thing in the company, we're preventing growth, and we're not teeing up our team members for success.

The other thing to remember is that you don't have to give away everything at once. In fact, you probably shouldn't. Start with something that's easy to give up: the thing you hate doing. Every leader has some part of the work that they aren't good at, don't like doing, and wish they could give away. So give it away.

The relief will be immediate. You'll find yourself more energized for work and with more time to devote to the work that only you can do. In my experience, it will probably feel so good that you'll be motivated to give away something else.

For every kind of work, there is someone out there who is not only good at it, but also enjoys it. Sometimes, as leaders, we can assume that everyone feels the way we do. If I don't like accounting, or HR, or if I'm not good at project management, everyone else must feel the same. More likely, there's someone at your company who is watching you do it and itching to get their hands on it. Let them. It will be an act of compassion for yourself and for them.

KNOW WHAT YOU WANT

"Getting rich, having all the material possessions in the world, sex, drugs, and cheap thrills will make you happy if you can just get enough of them in the right combination": a quote from No one ever in the history of the world.

Giving away control requires knowing what you want and

where you add value in your company. If you don't know what you want, you're going to try to control every single little thing because you won't know where to focus.

Part of this is getting beyond money. If you run a company, of course you want it to be profitable. You want to support yourself and your family—and your team members, too. But if you think that what you want is money, that's a sign that you don't know what you want. What will bring you happiness? What do you want the money *for*?

Sometimes we can feel guilty as entrepreneurs if we say what we want, or about wanting too much. Who am I to say that I want to work a few hours a week in a construction company so that I can put more time and effort into business coaching? It's like we think we have to be in enough pain to justify getting what we want, as if people have to see us suffering, and then we'll be allowed to have what we want.

It can feel like we have to earn the right to be in charge, or to make a certain amount of money. If I admit that I want more time with my family, more freedom, more carefree time and less work, is that even allowed?

Figuring out what you want from your business and from your life is an act of self-compassion. If all you want is money, there's no end. You'll always want another zero, another digit on the bank balance. There's always potentially more money to be made.

As entrepreneurs, we seek freedom. How are you going to know when you've reached it? Freedom looks different for each of us, and of course it includes financial freedom. But financial freedom is reflected in what the money makes possible, whether that's buying your friends dinner, or being able to walk your kids to school every day and be fully present with them. Freedom doesn't just mean achieving the outcomes or goals we've set for ourselves; it's the ability to be present to experience them.

This book is an example. All the profits are going to suicide prevention, not to make me wealthier. What I want is for the world to be more compassionate, and for other people who are suffering like my brother did to have the help they need.

That's a much more powerful driver, and more satisfying to me in the end, than whatever amount of money it might bring me.

DISCOVERY EXERCISE: WHAT CAN I GIVE AWAY?

This one is simple.

Write down a list of everything you're in charge of in your business, from developing the five-year plan to paying the electric bill every month. Anything you personally touch, write it down. Be honest.

Once you've done that, go back over the list. What can you hand over to someone else? What doesn't actually need to be done at all? What would someone else do better? As you look at all your tasks:

- **Put a D next to anything you can delegate**
- **Write "me" next to anything you think you're unique at and need to do**

Now take a look at the "D" tasks and write down all your objections or worries about giving those things away. Do you need to build trust with members of your team? Do you need to train someone or hire someone? What would it take to give that work away?

Then commit to taking some steps toward taking these items off your plate. You don't have to give it all up at once. A few small steps at a time will make a big difference—and the more you do it, the more you'll want to.

If you're having a lot of trouble with this exercise or really struggle giving work away, step back and do this exercise first:

Write down the last thing you thought you had control over, whether that was at work, at home, or in your life. Did you really control it? What parts of it, or what outcomes, could you totally control?

One of the hardest things for me to give up control over was employee retention. I think that I can control whether my best employees stay or leave, but I can't. That's not to say that I have no impact—far from it. Treating them well will make them much more likely to stay. But if they get a better offer, or if their son wants them to work from the beach, they're going to go.

It's hard at first, but every time I've let go of the belief that I can control some outcome, my stress has gone down—and generally, the outcomes get better because I'm focused on what I can do, rather than what I want to happen.

5

INVESTING IN COMPASSION

When my dad was still running the company, one of the super-intendents came to my dad and told him that his father was sick.

My dad didn't hesitate. He said, "Take a truck, and come back when he's better." Our company is in North Carolina, and the superintendent needed to get to New York. My dad let him take a company truck to drive up there and told him to stay as long as he needed. People in the company still talk about it, years later.

This is one of many areas where I very much strive to follow my dad's lead. When one of my team members came to me and told me he was facing a serious health issue, I told him to take all the time he needed to get better. I kept paying his salary and his health benefits.

While he was out for several months, he called me every week, worried about how his projects were going and the financial burden he was putting on the company. I told him, "We've got it covered. You get well and come back when you can." It took nearly six months before he could come back to his job.

I don't think I have to tell you that when he came back, his loyalty was unbreakable. He told me, "As long as you want me, I'm here." Great leaders have always known this. Alexander the Great, for one, knew that you have to share the wealth. He was well known for his generosity in distributing the spoils of war among his generals and his soldiers, and for taking care of the populations he conquered and being generous with them. He was even strategically generous with rivals and potential partners. He used generosity as a way to spread his influence and was incredibly compassionate in that regard.

The goal isn't to buy loyalty, but caring about people and showing it in a way that anyone can understand has a material impact on their lives.

Investing financially in people matters. Money has energy. When you hoard it, it loses that energy, but when you share it, the energy expands and works for you. And that investment isn't made just by you as the owner or leader of the company. When a leader takes six months off to get well, the whole team invests their time and effort in covering the work.

Why would they do that? Because they know, "This could happen to me. I might need the same compassion someday." It's the exact opposite of the "not my job" mentality you often see in bigger businesses.

This kind of compassion is a competitive advantage for entrepreneurs and small business owners. Think about the last time you dealt with a big company. When you call them up, it's pretty clear they don't care about you. Compare that to when you called a mom-and-pop business and got the owner, or when someone spent twenty minutes on the phone helping you figure something out. I know I'd rather pay a little more than sit on hold for six hours.

Some large companies can't or won't invest in compassion because they are overly focused on quarterly profits alone. Entrepreneurs, on the other hand, understand that this is for the long term. The work we're doing is for my family, and for the more than three dozen people who work for me and their families. I know all those people individually, and they know me. They're here working toward the same vision for the company that I have—or at least, that's how it can be.

We have the ability, as entrepreneurs, to do things differently, and that includes treating people differently and investing in them in unusual ways. It's shockingly and saddeningly rare, though, how often I see people doing this. Entrepreneurs can reinvent entire markets and not see the potential for reinventing how they treat the people right in front of them.

That's not a judgment. I had an amazing role model in this, my dad, and it still took me time to figure out how to do it myself. We invest in things that offer a return on investment, but all too often, we don't think about how investing in people can matter, and might offer the greatest return of any investment. Because it doesn't just return value in terms of money and profitability; it returns exponentially in terms of the caring, commitment, and loyalty of the people around you.

LEADERS EAT LAST, BUT THEY PUT THEIR OWN MASK ON FIRST

Sometimes it can seem like leaders get two very different messages. On the one hand, we hear about self-compassion and the idea that you should "put your own mask on first," referring to the instructions passengers are given when a plane encounters turbulence. Putting on your own oxygen mask first ensures that you have the capacity to help others.

But on the other hand, we're also told, in Simon Sinek's famous book, that "leaders eat last," suggesting that we should meet everyone else's needs first.

The key to understanding investing in people as a form of compassion is that a strong culture is one that can square these two concepts. In other words, you have to do both, but they relate to different parts of the business. Putting your own mask on first means putting the organization first, and "leaders eat last" is about compensation and rewards.

Another way to think of it is that eating is a reward, but you have to put your mask on to physically survive and be able to do things.

Putting your own mask on first is all the work we've talked about up to now: having compassion for yourself, doing the journaling or meditation or whatever other personal work you need to do to show up in a way that serves your needs and your business. It includes everything you do to be able to keep showing up as a leader and taking the business where it needs to go, including letting go of the work others can do so that you can lead.

Eating last is about results. Results come from everyone's hard work, not just mine. So when it comes time to "eat," or to share in the good stuff that comes from that hard work, I should put myself last.

For me, that means that I don't calculate my percentage until I've taken bonuses out. It might look different for you. This chapter will cover a number of different approaches. But no matter what your specific situation, being a leader requires you to see, value, and compensate the work of others before you take the credit, or the profits, for yourself.

Compassion is a personal journey, but it also has to be reflected in how you invest your time, energy, and resources in the people around you.

Sometimes people ask me why it matters that the investment is financial. Why not "attaboys" or company picnics? All I can say is, would you do all the work to grow your business 20 percent if all you got out of it was somebody telling you, "Great job?" Maybe you like to be told you're doing a good job. We all do. But you're running the business for profit.

Money is what puts food on the table. It sends kids to college and puts down payments on family homes. Investing in your people financially tells them that you see them as full human beings with needs and lives and dreams like yours, and that you understand they are working to fulfill those things for themselves. They might like you—and if you treat them with compassion, they're more likely to. But they're not working for you because they like you. They're working because they want and need things for themselves and their families. Investing in them financially shows that you support them on that deeper, human level, and that you see how their efforts contribute to your own financial success.

It's a way of showing them that you see them as equals. Isn't that the boss you would want to work for?

PUT YOUR MONEY WHERE YOUR VALUES ARE

Investing in compassion is also a way of showing your commitment to your core values. You can talk about values all day, but your team is only going to believe it if they see it. They watch where you put your time, energy, and focus—and your money.

If I want my team to live and breathe the values, I have to go first.

In my construction company, the first of our core values is "trustworthy." I've got to be able to trust my team to do the work, even when I'm not standing there. But trustworthiness goes both ways. They have to trust me not to nickel and dime them over benefits—to not save money at their expense. They have to know that I'm going to find ways to benefit and lift up everyone in the company when we do well, like giving bonuses or other performance incentives.

We have never done layoffs in the history of the company. That includes COVID-19.

In the construction industry, it's common practice to hire for a job once you get it. You get the contract, then hire the people to complete it, not the other way around. That very often leads to a cycle of hiring and layoffs. That's not what I do. I hire people who are a good fit for the business. I train them. Then I get the right work for the team I've hired. I don't fire them when business slows down; I rely on our ability to go out and get more work based on our skills and our culture.

That means I am fully financially invested in each and every employee I bring on. They know that from day one, and it creates security for them and loyalty to the company.

Our second care value is being "dedicated," first to yourself and your family, then to your community, then to your team, and lastly to the company. Being dedicated to yourself, your family, and your community first requires you to be a whole person, at work and at home. And that makes me feel even better about investing in my team members financially because I know my investment is actually much bigger than that: I'm investing in a family and in my own community as well.

We also value "belief in self," meaning that you have the maturity to execute your work once you're trained to do it and the wisdom to raise your hand when you don't know, and ask the question. Pretending to know stuff in the construction industry isn't just a weakness, it's dangerous. We have to know that our team is capable, and also capable of asking for help.

Finally, we value being "entrepreneurial and innovative." We're not a big company. You can't sit at your desk—or in your job site trailer—for eight hours and go home. I've seen people sit in their cars drinking coffee right until the clock hits 8am before they come into the office, and those people aren't for us. Definitely no clock watchers! We're all in, and we need people who bring solutions to the table.

Our company lives by these core values. They aren't just words on a poster. I hear people in meetings bring up values when they make decisions all the time. When I hire someone, I always give them the same talk. I tell them, this is a place where we care about each other, and these values are how we care about each other.

We take this so seriously that someone actually left the company because of the priority of these core values, because there wasn't alignment between them and the company. A few weeks after they were brought on board, they came to me and said, "If I'd known you were serious about all this stuff beforehand, I wouldn't have taken the job." They just wanted to do their job and go home, and that's not how we work.

So how does this relate to investing in compassion? We recognize that we're asking a lot from the people who work for us. We don't want clock punchers; we want people who are invested in our values on a deeper level. That puts the responsibility on us to invest in them in return.

Of course I don't suggest bankrupting the company to pay bonuses. That doesn't serve anyone. The more meaningful kind of investment is the day-in, day-out investments in showing people that you care about them. Benefits are one example. We want to have the best benefits we can because then we'll get the best employees. So when we look at our investment in benefits, we say, "The tie goes to the employee." If healthcare premiums go up and the company has to pay a little more for the employees to get the same benefit or cost, that's what we'll do.

How much you can invest in your employees, and how you make that investment (whether it's bonuses, or benefits, or something else) will look different for every entrepreneur. It will, and should, change from year to year. It's an issue of doing what you can, when you can.

When we have highly profitable years, we give out bonuses based on performance and results. Compassion is giving out bonuses during tough times. The team understands that we're investing in them as much as we can, while also maintaining the business that supports all of us.

In the end, what matters is showing compassion and caring for your people through your financial actions. You're going to attract better people, and those people are going to care more about, and be more loyal to, you and your company. When you take care of people, they will take care of you—and your clients—and the business will thrive.

YOU HAVE TO MEAN IT

It might seem counterintuitive, but the financial investment in people only works if you are also invested in them personally and emotionally. If you are investing in team members financially but not showing them compassion personally, they are apt to feel like you're underinvesting in them.

Imagine a team member who gets a bonus but hasn't gotten a compassionate word from his leader in months. He probably doesn't feel like he's seen as a person on a daily basis, and he doesn't know whether you care about him or not. When he gets a bonus check, he's likely to think, *If this is the amount they sent me out of nowhere, I bet they could have sent me more*, instead of *"Wow, this is great! Man, am I grateful to work at a company where my efforts are compensated, and I'm treated as a person and appreciated as a human being.* That's the feeling we hope to create in all our team members.

Without a genuine connection, he doesn't have any reason to believe you're doing the best, or the most, for him that you can. The compensation, however high it might be, becomes just a number, and they focus on that number because it's all the information they have.

Conversely, the smallest reward is far more powerful when you have an authentic connection with someone and they know that you are doing, and will do, as much as you possibly can for them. Remember, compassion is a two-way street. If you show compassion for them, you will get it back. They're more likely to give you the benefit of the doubt and say, "Even in a tough time, I'm still getting this amount."

Investing in people compassionately also means that you're not investing in them just to get a specific result. Yes, it creates loyalty. Yes, people are more likely to stay and work hard for you when you invest in them. But it's not a quid pro quo. When the team member came to me and said he was going to go work with his son on the beach, I didn't get annoyed about all the years I'd given him nice bonuses. Those investments weren't a waste just because he eventually left.

You're investing in people to invest in them, not turning them into a commodity. That is what being trustworthy looks like.

YOU SHOULD FEEL IT

One of the things to consider when you're thinking about investing in people, especially around bonuses, is exactly how much to give. I'm not going to give you a specific answer to that. What I do want to address is the fear that comes from investing in people, even in a bad year.

A couple of years ago, we had a pretty bad year, and I still gave out bonuses. We didn't have as much to give out as we'd hoped, but I gave out higher bonuses than the company had earned. Most of the net profit from that year, I gave out in bonuses. That was an unusual situation. In general, I stick to the motto that "You can't spend 'try,'" and the bonuses we give out reflect our actual results. COVID-19 changed the economics: our results weren't down because of our team or our effort, but because of an unprecedented worldwide shutdown. I looked at the situation holistically, saw that the future looked bright and that the work we were doing was very high-quality, profitable work, and I chose to invest in the efforts of my team.

Don't get me wrong. It wasn't every dime we had. In fact, it was money we had already allocated for bonuses. But it hurt.

And it should hurt. There should be a little bit of pain when you invest fully in people. That's how you know you're making a meaningful investment. This is also an area where the response is exponentially greater than the input. If you feel the pinch even a little bit, your team is going to feel it a lot.

Whatever amount of pain we feel in making the investment, the recipients will feel ten times that in compassion and love. On the other hand, if it's nothing to us, it's going to be nothing to them.

If you invest in them when times are hard, they'll feel that love even more. We show who we really are when times are tough, not when times are good. Leaders who hoard their profits during lean years are broadcasting to their teams that they are mostly focused on themselves, not on the company or the team, and that they're only willing to share when they won't have to feel it.

The reality about wealth that it took me a long time to understand is that the allocation of wealth conveys feelings. Our financial generosity, or more accurately our recognition, can convey caring and loyalty and trust and all the other values we care about, but only if we give enough to feel it ourselves. When you have to say to yourself, "I'm giving this much even though it's hard, because they earned it, and I care about them," that's a sign that you're making an investment that will also feel significant to them.

There are caveats to this, of course. If someone is underperforming, it's not compassionate to other people on the team to share the wealth equally with them. Showing love financially to someone who isn't performing doesn't promote your values. It undermines the focus on results and can demoralize others on the team.

There are also people out there who will not feel good about what you're giving them, no matter what. There's not enough money in the world for them to be grateful to you. As an entrepreneur, you will come across people who are entitled and think they deserve what they didn't earn. Some people think this is specific to the young "Zoomers" generation, but it's not; that kind of entitlement has been around forever, and it will probably be around forever. Prejudice of any kind isn't compassionate, and it can keep you from seeing who is performing and getting results, and who isn't.

Whoever they are, the entitled people need to be coached out of your company. If money is a form of caring, don't shower it on people who can't or won't reciprocate or notice.

In general, though, investing in people is investing in the future of your company. It might hurt now, but it will help "future you." Use it as a way to keep the people around you who share your values and your commitment, and they will return the favor by investing their time, energy, and effort in making the company successful.

INVESTING IN YOURSELF

Investing in compassion isn't just about bonuses and compensation. Those are financial investments, and they are important, but your most important resource isn't actually money, it's time. As Napoleon said to his generals when they were asking for more time to get ready for a mission: "I can give you more of anything, but I can't give you more time."

Time is the only thing we can't make more of, yet as entrepreneurs we often treat it like it's our least valuable commodity. Giving yourself time is an investment in yourself that will pay off in greater compassion, and greater success, for your entire company.

As entrepreneurs, we don't talk enough about slowing down. We tend to move fast and push through barriers and keep going. To be truly compassionate, we have to slow down and take the time to think, reflect, and engage. Doing a little bit of this work is so much more meaningful than powering through and knocking on the doors of our businesses and our lives.

My daughter is the epitome of finding a way to slow me down. She has Down Syndrome, and she teaches me patience and compassion by showing me how to be patient and to live in the moment. She is such a loving human being, and all she wants to do is live right now, in this moment, all the time. If we could all be more like people with Down Syndrome, we might all be a lot happier. I apply the patience she teaches me every day.

To be a compassionate leader means being a great coach, to help people get more out of themselves, not tell them what to do. Coaches help other people become champions. That means being a great learner as well as a great trainer. Even just taking time away to think about yourself, your role, and where you should be focusing your energy can pay big dividends in your willingness to coach because you'll be able to let other people take over areas you shouldn't be focusing on.

Some of the investments I've made in my own growth would have surprised my younger self. After my brother died, I came up against some realizations about myself. I saw that I was already a successful entrepreneur. I was already doing the physical fitness work and staying healthy. Where I had room for growth, and where I needed the most help, was my mental health. Even getting to that realization required me to take time, look honestly at myself, and develop some self-awareness.

When I could step back and see where I needed to do work, I invested in therapy and started working through things that had been sitting inside me for a long time. I went to a transcendental meditation retreat, despite the nagging feeling that I shouldn't be leaving the company in other people's hands for that long. I worried that I'd lose the respect of the team if I wasn't there beside them, working longer days than everyone else.

What happened was the exact opposite. Every one of those investments in myself made me a better leader. Since I've started taking time for this work on myself, I've seen my team become more receptive to me. My interactions with my leadership team are better and more respectful in both directions. Our relationships are better.

I've got a huge issue I'm working on right now that could end up being a multi-million dollar problem, and my integrator and I are joking around and laughing about it. Before, I would have been so laser-focused on the issue that I wouldn't have seen the things he was bringing to the table. We would have gotten, at best, the same result, but with tons of stress and me feeling like I had to control everything. Now I can step back and relax because I know he knows what he's doing, and I am self-aware enough to see when I'm getting controlling. We're actually having *fun* at work, even when there are big issues to work through.

If the one thing I can't make more of is time, then spending time with people I like, who I can have fun with, who I have good relationships with, instead of constant conflict, is a huge return on investment.

The other reason to invest in yourself is to model it for your team. When we're not investing in ourselves, we're much less likely to do it for others, and we're showing the people around us that we don't think that kind of work is important. There's almost an element of proving that you mean it. If you believe investing in people, in compassion, and in relationships is important, you'll do it yourself first. If you say you take care of people, but you don't take care of yourself, people won't believe you.

Even with my dad, I saw this happen. He was one of the most generous people I've ever met. He took care of other people all the time, but he didn't take care of himself. If he had a really good day, he'd have a couple of drinks and smoke some cigarettes to celebrate, and if he had a bad day, he'd have a bunch of drinks and smoke a few cigarettes to feel better. I've got a lot of that in me, too. When things are stressful, I can find myself drinking more than I want to and falling into the habit of not taking care of myself.

As a leader, those actions have far-reaching impact. People look at how you treat yourself to see if it lines up with your words. If your actions aren't in concert with the claims you're making about yourself as a leader, or as a person, it comes off as inauthentic. In addition, it can seem to people like maybe you mean well, but you don't actually know how to take care of people. Everything you do as a leader is read by your team as proof (or disproof) of what you say you believe.

And there's the tough reality, too, that if you don't take care of yourself, you might not be able to take care of others. My dad died of a stroke at sixty-one. He's not around now to take care of the people he loved. Watching him, I learned that you have to take care of yourself so that you can continue to care for others. That's what I want to do for my family and for my team.

So now, instead of having a few extra drinks after a hard week, I remember that the bad weeks are building blocks for future good weeks. When I take the time to look at that and learn from it, to invest in my own mental health instead of wallowing in distractions, everyone benefits.

INVESTING IN THE BUSINESS

The final piece of investing in compassion is investing in the business itself, which can mean anything from leadership training to operating systems and platforms.

One of my own struggles in leadership has been responding to negative feedback. Like a lot of entrepreneurs, I can be a perfectionist, and for a perfectionist, negative feedback hits hard. In the past, when I've gotten negative feedback, I haven't always responded well, and it's sometimes held the entire company back.

I remember in the military, one of the comments I would get

was that I was not open to constructive criticism. Unfortunately, it was almost impossible for me to learn from that feedback because—I wasn't open to it. I'd walk away from it thinking, "They said I'm not open to feedback, that's bullshit."

It's hard to get through to someone when they're in that kind of self-reinforcing cycle.

I've had to learn that it's not just good for me to hear the truth; it's a huge and important boon for my company when I, as the leader, get accurate feedback and can act on it. When I'm open to being coached, when someone holds up a mirror to let me see how my behavior is affecting the whole business, and I act on it, the whole company gets better. And that applies to my entire leadership team. Investing in that kind of feedback and coaching can have big returns for the success of your business.

The value of those kinds of investments is even higher in a business like mine. We're in construction. It's a service. We don't make widgets. Of course we invest in equipment and all that, but at the core, the company is the team. The people are the company.

The way a teammate interacts with a client can have more impact on our bottom line than the biggest capital investments we ever make. Conversely, investing in making the company run more efficiently and effectively is a compassionate act because it allows you to focus on the things that matter, including people. You can maximize the brain power you're using and not waste people's talents or time. So for us, investing in people is investing in the company—and investing in the company is investing in people.

I'm an EOS™ Implementer and coach—and a believer in it as a system. I'm not going to sell you on EOS. That's not the point of this book.

But before running the business on an operating system that

is simple and clear and that defines how often we meet and how to run our meetings (and more), we were definitely wasting a lot of talent and time. It was like that old myth that people only use seven percent of their brain. The actual fact is that we only know what 7 percent of the brain does. Imagine that. We use 100 percent of our brain, but we only clearly understand what 7 to 10 percent of it does! I've always wondered whether part of that other 93 percent is our understanding of how to be communal, our dependence on each other, and the importance of compassion. If so, companies are often missing that same part of the picture.

Running on an operating system is like getting to see and master the other 93% of the company's brain. We're able to utilize everyone's highest and best efforts.

When my dad passed away, I knew there was no way I could lead the company the way he did. He had forty years of experience in the field, and I was never going to have that. I looked around the company, though, and realized that there were plenty of people already on the team who had significant experience that could help supplement this loss. I was able to say, "Okay, my dad was able to run the company that way, but I'm not." Instead, I saw that there was somebody who was really good at finances, and someone else who was great at operations, and I could find the right people to fill any gaps. EOS® offered a system for making use of, and valuing, all of these different contributions.

There's a parallel to the military in some ways. The military has a natural structure to it, where people have a certain specialty. That specialty provides clarity and defines everything you do. The result is that you respect each person's part in the whole—and you make more money for everyone to share, which fuels the ability to invest in people financially and creates a cycle of trust and loyalty.

SCALING UP COMPASSION

The beauty of the compassionate approach is that it naturally scales itself. All you have to do is start it.

In the beginning, when you're running a three- or four-person company, you can take care of all of them yourself. As your business grows, though, the number of people you can successfully engage with in a meaningful way doesn't change. Studies of indigenous tribes and the military have found that five is the magic number: if you can be compassionate and take great care of the five most influential leaders in your company, they will do the same for the five people closest to them—and compassion in your organization will spread like wildfire, and spread outward to your clients as well.

There are still some construction company clients I invest in personally, but more and more, I trust the small circle of people I directly manage to take that investment outward. I can see the results in the way my frontline people represent me and the company. They are out there in the field reflecting the same values, and the same care for others, that I am showing my leadership team at the top.

And while it's true that compassion can't be just a tactic—that it won't work unless you really mean it—the good news is that authentic compassion also has powerful benefits on the business side.

DISCOVERY EXERCISE: HOW MUCH CAN I INVEST IN MY TEAM?

When I first started doing this, I thought of my team members as a cost. There was even some resentment about giving out bonuses—and not always hearing "thank you" when I did. But my thinking has evolved, and now I realize that my team members are not a cost. They're an investment. Investing in them is a way of thinking about, and planning for, the future of my company.

I'm also investing in a relationship, showing them that I authentically care about their well-being and appreciate their contribution to our shared success.

So the question now isn't whether I should invest in them—it's how much. What percentage of my profit will I share with the people who make it happen? What is your projected revenue, and what will your profits look like if you invest a percentage of that revenue?

When you've decided how much you plan to invest, make a commitment. Pick a number, a percentage of your net profit, that you will distribute to the team, and commit to it. I don't share that number with my team, but I know. That way, I'm not swayed by feelings of scarcity when the time comes to give the bonuses; I've already decided.

6

THE BENEFITS OF COMPASSION

In 2022, my wife took our eight-year-old son to his first flag football game, and when she got home, I could see that something was wrong.

"It was a mess," she said. "The coach is terrible. He was yelling at them, it was bad." In fact, it was so bad that the team was looking for almost anyone who was willing to become the coach. My wife said, "You should do it."

At the time, I didn't know anything about football. But from what she told me about the toxic nature of the coach, I knew it was going to be a problem for my son, and the rest of the kids, if he stayed on. I agreed to do it.

The first day I met with the kids, we started with a name game and got to know each other. I may not know football, but I knew enough about leadership and compassion by that point that I knew we had to start with caring about each other, especially after their experience with the other coach. We spent some time on that, and then I gathered them up and set the vision for the team.

"Okay," I told them. "Here's the deal. We're going to run right every single play until we're up by two touchdowns. Then the quarterbacks can pick any play they want."

They asked who was going to be the quarterback, and I said, "Everybody will get to be everything. Every four downs, we'll rotate. Everyone will get a chance to be the quarterback, and the running back, and everything else."

So that's what we did. They'd run right for four downs in a row, then rotate, then run right again, and rotate again. We practiced this for maybe ten minutes, and then that's all we did the entire season.

They didn't lose a single game.

The other coaches in the league were out there on the field with two to five coaches for each team, waving clipboards and yelling plays to the players on the field. The coaches looked incredibly frustrated, and the kids looked confused by the complex plays the coaches were drawing up. While that was going on, I just stood on the sidelines cheering on my team because they had everything they needed to do it themselves. They were empowered. They knew the results they needed to get, and they got them.

Everybody knew their role at any given time. They knew that they wouldn't always be the one to score the touchdown, but they also knew that they would get their chance—and the credit—when it was their turn.

Now, it's true that this approach was partly (or maybe mostly) born out of my limited knowledge of football. But it was also based on my understanding and caring for them as people. Even kids understand the difference between a leader who prescribes every little move and the one who lets them use their own abilities. I told them, "It's your game to win or lose, not mine." I wasn't tied to the outcome, and that meant that they were the ones who won the games, and the ones who got to feel the pride of those wins.

The most important impact of that compassion was seeing them have fun out there and watching them grow as humans. The benefit—winning the games—was a byproduct of that. The same is true in business. If you see the benefits as the reason to be compassionate, you're not actually being compassionate. On the other hand, if you are compassionate because you care, you will see great benefits.

And there's something to be said for keeping things simple. That can be compassion, too.

HOW WE DO TRUMPS WHAT WE DO

There are a lot of business benefits to genuine compassion, and we'll get to those. But I want to step back and take a longer view for a minute.

Think about the end of your life. There have been studies about what people think and feel on their deathbeds. They never say, "I wish I'd landed those three clients" or "I wish I'd made that one deal." They don't think about the money they made or wring their hands that they didn't spend more hours at work.

They remember how people treated them—and how they treated people. They say, "I wish I'd spent more time with my family" and "I wish I'd been kinder."

My wife is a nurse, and she's heard the same things over and over. No one thinks about whether they were productive enough on their deathbed.

Far, far beyond the business benefits of compassion are

the human benefits, especially the feeling of having a positive impact on the people you care about and work with. That's why "how we do what we do" is so much more important than what we do.

I remember I had an amazing leader in the Army. It was a staff job in an infantry battalion, which is the S3 Air or Assistant S3. The S3 is the head planner for the battalion, who creates the plans for all the operations. The AS3 is basically that person's assistant. It was a planning job. At the time, we were planning a training mission. We built a lot of PowerPoint decks for the briefs and for the decision-making process.

It wasn't the kind of thrilling, high-stakes work you imagine when you think of military experience. But that leader made a more positive impact on me as a leader than many of the leaders I worked for in more demanding missions.

Whatever we were doing, he cared. He wanted us to do it well, and to know that he cared about us as people and about our success. I'm still friends with him to this day. Long after all your business deals are done, that's the kind of impact that matters.

Of course, right now, in the midst of running your company, other benefits are important, too. The power of compassion is that doing the right thing, for the right reason—caring about people just to care about them—also paves the way for better outcomes.

BEST IN CLASS

A few years ago, my construction company proposed for a project we weren't sure we were going to get. It was a big project, a building envelope renovation with a lot of unusual elements. There were thirty-eight separate phases in the plan we outlined for them, there would be a lot of night and weekend work, and it was a complex project.

When they called us to say we won the job, they told us, "You weren't the lowest price. You weren't even *near* the lowest price. But you knew the project better than anyone else, and everyone who visited the site was incredibly professional."

I was happy to get the project—but I wasn't surprised. By that time, I knew the value of the way we work. When we went to the site visits prior to pricing the project, we asked insightful questions and offered unique solutions. The client could tell that we knew what we were doing.

But what set us apart most, and what sold the client despite the higher bid, was that it wasn't just me as the owner showing up with these good questions and ideas. It was the whole team. A lot of companies send the owner to do the initial site visits, and in a company with more than ten people, pretty much everyone on the client side knows the owner of the construction company is never going to see this project again. Instead, I sent the team that was going to do the work, so the client knew that this was the team they were going to get. And every single person from our team who showed up to the site had the same attitude because of the way we live our core values and commit to each other.

Even the client could see it. They told us, "We could tell they all really cared about what you do, your reputation, and our project."

In the end, it paid off for them, too. We got the job done faster than expected, and they saved 20% off the time they projected for completion.

We are sought after because we take good care of our people. Clients can feel the difference: team members who are well taken care of will take care of clients better, too. The compassion we show our team internally translates directly into our team's compassion and caring for clients on the project. The leadership doesn't have to show up to the site because every person in our company lives these values every day, and clients can see that.

When your people see how much you care about them and about the work, they take that into everything they do, and the result is a best-in-class product or service. Somebody who's not world-class at what they do is going to try to compete on price, but when your service is better than everybody else, when it's visible how much your team cares about what they're doing, you no longer have to do that.

We can ask the price that our work is worth—and the side effect is that we end up only working with clients who also value compassion. That's a quality of life benefit that will have more impact on our day-to-day experience than even the money.

RECRUITMENT AND RETENTION

It's not just clients who are impressed by compassion and becoming more compassionate. You'll also see your difficulties in recruitment and retention nearly disappear. That's not to say no one will ever leave. I wrote about how one of my best people recently left after nearly twenty years to go work on the beach with his son. That happens, and to be honest, that's the kind of turnover I'm happy to see. There is all the difference in the world between someone leaving to fulfill a personal dream and the constant coming-and-going of employees that most companies deal with.

When we genuinely care about our people, our best team members are going to tell their friends. They'll be talking and say, "You know, I've worked for jerks before, but now that I've worked here, I'll never put up with that again." Their friends will hear about how different it is to work for you, and they'll want to come on board, too.

Even better, the people who work for you will care about your mission, and in my experience, that means they're only going to invite in others they think are going to make a real contribution. They won't want to spoil a good thing by bringing in team members who won't fit the culture.

At this level, recruitment and retention become less about money and more about relationships. The money will always be there because the product and service are world class. The financial rewards for both the entrepreneur and the team will always be there because we're investing in our teams. And the team will always be there because people know when they've got a good thing going. It's a self-fulfilling prophecy.

I know this is true because I see it every day. We've got parents and children working together in our construction company. We've got people who have recruited their best friends. That, to me, is the ultimate compliment. When somebody brings their kid or their best friend into the company, we know we're treating people well. We also know that both of them are less likely to leave in the future, as long as we keep treating them well.

Over time, the more we lead this way, the less the company works like a group of strangers and the more it becomes a community, with everyone contributing to make it better. Including clients.

CLIENT RELATIONSHIPS

Compassion is what I'd call a 10x for client relationships.

The reality of running a company, at least once it gets past the one-or-two-person startup phase, is that we as the owners can't possibly interact with every client. We have eleven superintendents dealing with all kinds of projects. They have more impact on the relationship with the client than I ever can.

If I take good care of those superintendents, they take care of the clients. It's that simple. And it has a lot more impact. When clients see and hear company values from the owner, they tend to write them off. Of course the owner is going to say those things. When they see and hear it from everyone on the team, consistently, in every interaction, then they start to understand that this is something special—that we mean it.

That's when they start calling you over your competitors.

COMPETITORS GO AWAY

You might think that every construction company offers essentially the same services. But that's a scarcity mindset, a belief that the available work is a limited pie you have to compete for against other basically identical companies.

The reality, which took me a long time to realize, is that there is nobody who does what I do.

I could tell everyone in the world exactly what I do and how I do it, and it wouldn't matter. They will still never be me, and they can't do what I do, even if they think they understand what it is. What you have to offer above your basic services is *you*.

Many consultants or business coaches ask: "What's the competition doing?" My team and I very rarely think about the competition. Sometimes, sure, if we're pricing a project, we'll ask ourselves, "Where did we land?" But most of the time, what the competition is doing is just not relevant—so much so that it's almost like there is no competition.

When we think about ourselves in terms of how we're going to look more like the competition, that's the opposite of self-compassion. It's like we're putting ourselves away and saying, "I'm not going to be me, I'm going to be in these boxes that other people want me to check." We might as well be telling ourselves outright that who we actually are isn't valuable, when actually, the only person you can effectively be is yourself.

Also, when we think about how we're going to beat the competition, we put ourselves into a very narrow and specific box instead of thinking about the circumstances unique to that project or our unique potential.

After my dad passed away, I was told by a lot of people that I needed to learn to be a project manager. As the new owner, they said, that was my role in the business now. That's how a lot of my competitors in the industry run their businesses and how they see their place in their companies. I was new to running the business, so I listened.

I ran the company that way for a year, and I hated it. I'd get home, and all I could think was, "I hope this isn't what my life is going to be from now on."

It's not that I can't be successful as a project manager. I can. But it would be incredibly painful because I wouldn't be playing to my strengths. When I had to project manage every day, it exhausted me. My strengths are way on the other side of the scale. I'm a coach and a leader, an entrepreneurial thinker and a strategist. Every day I spent as a project manager drew heavily on my weaknesses and left my strengths dormant.

I'd built a career of misery, and I kept doing it because I thought that's what I was supposed to be doing.

A year of that was all I could take. In the end, I hired project managers and let them do what they do well. It took a surprising amount of guts to do that because even a lot of my advisors were saying, "What are you doing? You need to be a PM in your company to keep an eye on what's happening."

Now I stay high-level and get to focus on what I'm great at—or at least what I'm passionate about—which is leadership and big, interesting new opportunities. I leave the day-to-day to other people, and that lets me build a coaching business—and write this book—instead of going in and managing construction projects day in and day out. I love getting projects in the door, but then I hand it off to someone else who brings it in on time and on budget. And even that has gotten to a point where I'm delegating the sales and marketing more often. My team loves to see me let go because they've got it.

A lot of entrepreneurs think they have to have a certain role in their business, and they struggle hard to fit into it. What I learned was that I needed to have compassion for myself to embrace what I was good at. I finally asked myself, "If there's someone else who is better at doing something I hate doing, why am I still doing it?"

Maybe you're in the sales seat, or the finance seat, or the operations seat, and you can tell you're not doing it well or that you hate it. If you can find someone else to do that work, it gives you more time and capacity to do what you're good at and enjoy. This is compassion for yourself and for the people you hire, who love that work.

I get that this is hard. You've built this business, or you've owned it and been running it this way for a long time. Maybe you're afraid of what will happen if someone else doesn't do it the way you would. This is a tough thing to do, and we have to find the right people first, before we can let go.

When you start out as a new entrepreneur and it's just you, maybe you can't offload everything you don't want, but as soon as you can, it's a gift to yourself and to the company to do it.

That's also when the competition starts to disappear. Because you're no longer offering a service that looks just like everyone else's in a company that operates just like everyone else's. A competitor is someone who could potentially offer a client the same service. By that definition, I don't have any competitors. I'm the only person in the world who can do exactly what I do, who runs my business exactly the way I run it, who shows up with my values and my way of caring for people.

Clients can see that, and they respond to it.

FINANCIAL SECURITY

The financial security that comes from running your business compassionately isn't only based on the ability to attract clients or retain employees. The underside of the business is theft and loss. Employee theft is estimated to cost American businesses as much as $50 billion every year.

In the construction business, there's theft of tools, equipment, and materials. There are also losses that can come from shoddy work or dangerous conditions.

Compassion is an amazingly powerful antidote to these problems.

People steal from people they don't respect. They don't steal from people they care about. A good example of this is malpractice suits. The doctors who get sued are the ones with the worst bedside manner and the ones who are rude to patients, not the ones who make the most severe mistakes. That's a powerful demonstration that "how we do" trumps "what we do."

We essentially don't have to worry about theft anymore. The same applies to other kinds of loss. Our team cares a lot about each other, about the work, and about the clients because we consistently show that we care about them. That kind of caring reduces safety hazards and halfhearted work, which can amount to huge losses and terrible accidents in our business.

Honestly, it goes back to kindergarten. Just be nice. It's amazing how far that can go.

MORE THAN JUST A JOB

One of the best benefits of compassion, for me, is the feeling that I get when I come into work. It's the feeling that everyone there sees this as more than just a job.

Many companies have the "Where's Bill?" mentality. The leadership is constantly asking where everyone is and what they're doing. If my team is hitting their numbers, I don't give a shit where they are. I'm not a hall monitor. We're not keeping attendance.

When we're not compassionate, we have to take attendance because it's the only way to know that people aren't taking advantage of us. The problem is, that's not performance. That's control. It's the mindset that people are stealing from us whenever they're not working, like if you're not here right now, you must be stealing from me.

Noncompete agreements work the same way. I don't need noncompetes because I don't lose employees to competitors all the time—because I treat them with compassion. Noncompetes feel to me like companies that try to make a profit by making it hard to cancel their service. Noncompete agreements are scarcity minded: "I'm afraid I'm going to lose you, I'm afraid of what we're going to do if you're not here, and I'm afraid of the value you might bring to another company."

If somebody doesn't want to work for you, let them go. You're better off without them! When we attract the people we need, the ones who are great fits, they'll love working with us. Why insult them with a noncompete?

The opposite of that is saying, "I care about you, and I trust you. I hired you to do a job, and you're hitting your numbers every week, so keep it up."

What happens when we work this way is that people take pride in their work. It's no longer just a job. They don't feel like they're putting in the contractually obligated amount of time to get a paycheck.

I have to spend a lot of time with these people and at this company. Walking into a building where people are proud to be there, want to be there, and are committed to the work and each other changes my entire experience. I don't dread it. I'm not surrounded by conflict. I don't have to track anybody down or wonder whether they are cheating me. That's worth a lot.

EVERYTHING IS MAGNIFIED IN A SMALL BUSINESS

You'll see these benefits of compassion whether you're leading a small company or a large one, but the impact of every interaction is magnified in a small business—and for the same reasons, the effects are larger.

In the Army, there was a saying that "as long as you don't get a DUI or get arrested, you're going to get promoted." Larger organizations sometimes operate like this. Smaller companies can't. Their very survival depends on being effective and hitting targets. In a bigger organization, it can be harder to pin down where specific results come from, and where losses are happening. It's like being in an ocean liner. It can be hard to spot a hole.

In a company of thirty people, it's immediately obvious where the holes are.

As entrepreneurs, every single word we say matters. Our team is listening to every word we say, and when the team is small, each word is that much more impactful. We need to be thoughtful and considerate with the language we use if we want to inspire them.

Sports psychology provides a good model for emphasizing the positive over the negative. "Away motivation" is when a person is motivated "away from" doing something, or to *not* do it. I think about that when I hire, and I don't hire people who have "away" motivation for changing jobs. If I ask them why they're looking for work, and they say, "I don't want to be in the medical industry anymore" or "I don't like my current job," I don't hire them. I want people on my team with positive motivations, and I try to hold myself to the same standard.

The impacts of your leadership on a small team are similarly much more immediate and obvious in a small company. As entrepreneurs, we can take advantage of these benefits, and make a significant impact on our teams, by making even small, incremental movements in the direction of greater compassion. Every decision and every interaction has a more powerful effect on the whole.

DISCOVERY EXERCISE: WHO AM I GRATEFUL FOR?

I've talked a lot about the leaders I worked for in the Army—many fantastic and a few not so good. I don't remember all the jobs I did for them or everything we accomplished, but I absolutely remember how each one treated me. And the specific incidents I remember aren't big or showy. One leader I worked for would always say, "Thank you so much" whenever I did something for him. That's a very small thing, but it made me want to work even harder for him. I was always happy to do more if he needed it because he showed gratitude and appreciation.

Our entire culture is built on the law of reciprocity: it's human nature that when someone treats us well and bends over backward for us, we are going to do the same for them. We don't practice compassion or gratitude just to get something back, but the law of reciprocity reminds us that the way we treat people goes both ways. It's not just, "Who am I treating well," but "Who am I grateful to have in my life?" Committing to gratitude reminds us that relationships are at the basis of everything we do.

You don't have to do this exercise daily, but it can be especially powerful for those of us who sometimes fall into telling people what to do. Showing gratitude helps us remember their value and what they already know and are good at. It shifts us from the telling mindset to the trust and respect mindset and frees up both of us to do the work we do well.

Just keep in mind while you're doing it that, like all the other benefits of compassion, the loyalty and hard work you receive when you give gratitude is a byproduct. We all have to start with genuine compassion and genuine gratitude. Everything else follows from that.

Write down who you are grateful for in your life, personally and professionally, and specifically why you are grateful for them. What can you say or do to show them your gratitude?

7

THE GREATER GOOD

A few months after my dad died, while I was still dealing with grief and trying to learn the business, one of the people who worked for me came in, sat down in my office, and said, "Either you give me a huge payout right now, or I'm out."

It wasn't a case of, "I want a raise," or "I think I'm worth more." He was trying to extort me.

This particular employee was always on the point of leaving, with one foot out the door, even when my dad was still around. Then, when my dad died, he said he would stay to help me out. That didn't last long before he decided he could try to pressure me into paying him a huge amount of money to stay.

We had a really big project that we were chasing at the time, and he had a key role in our winning that project. He essentially told me, "Unless you pay me this amount of money, I won't do any more work. I've done enough for this company, and I deserve more."

I can't say I was stunned. He had always been the kind of

person who couldn't see the value of the team, only what he was doing. On any project he was on, he was always talking about what he did and what he accomplished, never what the team did. In his mind, every successful project he'd been a part of, he was the only reason for its success—and he should get the profits.

The part of me that still lives with a scarcity mindset felt like, "Maybe I should give in." It kept thinking, "What if I can't find anyone else? What work am I going to have to do if he leaves? How am I going to have time to add more to my own plate right now?"

Instead, I told him, "I'm letting you go."

He was furious. "Twenty years of service, and this is how you treat me? I've done so much for this company, and you repay me by firing me?" It's interesting, looking back, how little self-awareness he had. He was trying to extort me, and he was getting mad at me because it wasn't working. We're always the hero in our own story, I guess.

It was hard to stay calm, and honestly, nobody likes firing people. You shouldn't like firing people. It's a responsibility not to take lightly. But he'd quit four or five times before. He had shown his hand over and over again that he wasn't part of the team, that he didn't even recognize the team. He didn't share our values. He didn't care about whether the company was successful or profitable, only what was coming to him.

He didn't understand, at a basic level, the need for a team, or the need for people to take care of each other. I realized that if I gave in, there was no way it was going to stop here. He was going to keep wanting more, and he was going to see it as me admitting he was right, that the team couldn't work without him. That would have been a disaster. And if I gave in to his demands, no one else would get a bonus for years. We would be robbing everyone else to pay him off.

I decided that I wasn't going to have somebody hold me hostage in my own company, especially someone who was going to take advantage of me right after my dad passed away. It was an "easy wrong, tough right" situation because tolerating his behavior would have been easier in the short term—but in the long term, it would have been disastrous. The hard, right thing to do was to cut him loose, but there was pain in doing that, too.

When I was first running the company after my dad passed away, I fell into the snares that a lot of high-energy, ambitious entrepreneurs fall into, especially the "nobody cares, just shut up and work" approach that is the opposite of caring and compassion. Most of this book is about how to change that mindset. But compassion isn't just about being nicer. In fact, it's not really about being nice at all. It's about taking responsibility for the people you've chosen to work with, for, and around. That's what this chapter is about.

WHAT COMPASSION ISN'T

Genuinely caring about people is the key to compassion. That is very different from trying to make people like you.

I've seen leaders who thought they were taking a caring, compassionate approach, when in fact they were just trying to avoid conflict and be well liked. Compassion is not a popularity contest; it's about making the hard decisions and having the hard conversations, and it's about the greater good. That's a much harder task.

Compassion means not tolerating bad behavior, a toxic culture, or people who don't fit what you're trying to achieve. When someone on the team is hurting the business or holding everyone else back, it is an act of compassion to let them go. Trying to force them to fit when they don't would be a lack of compassion. The greater good takes into account the overall culture you're building, not one individual or one situation, and it's certainly not about avoiding tough decisions.

Making tough calls is part of being compassionate—for others, and also for yourself. Tolerating someone in my company who is trying to extort me at the expense of the rest of the team would have been a nightmare, and giving in to the entitlement mindset does not change behavior.

Our responsibility as leaders is to have compassion for everyone we've hired, all these people who rely on the company for their livelihoods and their families' support. If we care about them, they'll take care of everything else.

NO MR. NICE GUY

My wife is important to me for so many reasons, and one of them is that she tells me the truth about myself. One thing she's told me a few times is, "You're very kind, but you're not nice."

It might sound harsh at first, but it's true Nice means doing things in spite of yourself, letting people step on you because you don't want to make waves. Nice is avoiding short-term pain and, all too often, causing long-term problems as a result. When people say about a leader, "He's a really nice guy," I often find that nothing is getting done; he's being taken advantage of because of his "niceness."

Kind is different. Kind means that you will bend over backwards for the people who are in it with you. Kind is knowing that we're all in the boat together, and if the boat sinks, we're all going to drown, so we have to pull together. Kind means holding the door open for people and being compassionate to strangers just because we can. At its best, kindness is a recognition of shared humanity.

We are what we tolerate. If we tolerate poor performance from one or two people on the team, that will show the rest of the team that the new bar is at the level of the poor performer. As an entrepreneur who runs a small company, there are four or five dozen people in my boat. If all but one or two of them are really rowing hard, that's a problem—not just for me, but for everyone else who is doing the work. It might be "nice" to let that person sit around in the boat, but it's not kind.

The life-or-death nature of the military makes the distinction even more obvious. Being nice to a teammate who isn't carrying his weight could lead to someone getting killed. That's not an acceptable trade. As entrepreneurs, our impact isn't usually life-or-death, but we have people's careers and salaries in our hands, and the success of the company is prosperity for all of us.

Kindness means taking that responsibility seriously.

THEY ARE NOT YOUR FRIENDS

I love playing video games with my son. But that doesn't mean we're friends. Of course our employees aren't our kids. They're not children. There are similarities in that we care deeply about them and love them dearly—and being their friend is not productive or authentic.

Acting like a friend to your child robs them of something they need: the experience of having a loving and effective parent. Parenting isn't friendship because our children need something very different from us. They need coaching, guidance, protection, support, sustenance, and sometimes correction.

Our employees already have friends. What they need from us, as leaders, is something else.

We support our friends no matter what. When they tell

us about their problems, we usually take their side, no matter what the situation. We're fully in their court, almost like they can do no wrong.

Friendship is a form of safety. You take your friend's word at face value, and they can tell you about everything that's going on with them. Most of the time, you're not asking, "Well, what could you have done differently?" Sure, sometimes we have a difficult heart-to-heart with a friend, but most of the time, we reserve that. We listen, and we take their side.

The difference with leadership is the need for results. Even if we have to sit down with a friend and tell him something he doesn't want to hear, we're not invested in the outcome. He can do whatever he wants with his takeaways from our conversations. There's no communal or corporate goal. It's not a black-and-white difference. I care authentically about my friends and about my teammates. The difference is that a friend's decision doesn't generally impact my life. That might sound selfish, but as a leader, it's my responsibility to care about any action that could impact the team positively or negatively. As a friend, it's more often my responsibility to just listen and offer support.

We might call a friend just to vent sometimes, and that's healthy and normal, but that's not a leader relationship. You can pontificate with your friends. You can get a beer and let your guard down. As a leader, that's not going to serve the business or the employee. In fact, part of my work is to be respectful of their time so they can get the work done.

Sometimes it can seem like compassion to let an employee complain, or to complain to them. It feels like you're connecting. But that takes away from them something they need: a leader who helps them get the results that are required in their job.

And in the end, we aren't their friends, no matter how

friendly we are. This is where the power dynamic comes into play. We decide their salaries and bonuses. We can fire them or promote them. Friends are safe to complain to because they don't have any power over us. It's disingenuous for us as leaders to play that role.

It can be tempting to fall into black and white thinking about relationships: either I'm the jerk driving progress, or I'm the friend. There's nothing in between. I saw a similar debate in the Army. Should we care more about the men, or about the mission? If we put all our focus on the mission, we might allow ourselves to accept casualties needlessly, even flippantly. If we put the men first, we'll never go outside the wire. There has to be a balance.

Fortunately, we can like and care about and support people without being their friends—and that is what they need from us. We're working together to get certain results, and we serve them much better by helping them get those results than by wanting them to be our friends.

And let's be honest—no one wants to be friends with the boss.

LESS OF US IS MORE

In the military, units commemorate certain occasions with formal events, where the formation wears their best formal wear and brings spouses or partners. They're called military balls. At a military ball, everyone arrives in formal dress at the beginning of the night. That's when the Commander shows up. He walks around, shakes hands, stays for a brief period—and then leaves. And that's when the real party starts.

As long as he's there, the team or the subordinates have to be formal. They have to watch what they say and be on their best behavior. They're all more than a bit relieved when he leaves. But they would also be hurt if he didn't show up at all.

There are two ends to this spectrum. At one end is the cold, distant, "work is work" employer. He's the stereotypical hardass who says, "You're here to work. I don't care about anything else." That's not exactly endearing. No one wants to put in the extra effort for that person; in fact, their only motivation will be to work hard enough to get another job, away from them.

At the other end is the gladhander, the leader who walks around slapping everybody on the back, never pushing anybody, never asking tough questions, letting everyone get away with murder. He might be popular (although not necessarily), but nobody can count on him when things get tough, and he lets things slide that he should be dealing with.

There's a sweet spot in the middle that is compassion. Leaders are human, too, so we're not all the same. Some fall more to one side, some more to the other. There's no single spot on this spectrum that's right for everyone. But if our team members treat us like friends, and we aren't making hard decisions, we are too far toward the friend end of the spectrum.

Take a step back and think about what your own boundaries are as a leader. For myself, I have a rule that, as far as personal life is concerned, I let people share with me. They choose how much, or how little, to disclose about their life outside of work.

When a friend shares, it's never oversharing. You want to know everything they are dealing with, good and bad, and they want to know the same about you. There's reciprocity. Between a leader and a team member, it should not be reciprocal. The team member gets to choose what sharing looks like, and our role as leaders is not to reciprocate, but to listen and understand.

It's not always perfectly clear where the sweet spot is. If no one wants to tell us, as leaders, anything about who they are outside of work, we have probably gone too far toward "command and direct." Our doors need to be open for our team members to be able to share whatever they're comfortable with, personally and professionally, and we need to make space for that.

But when we find ourselves engaged in conversations in which we are oversharing, we've gone too far in the other direction. The example I always think of is Michael Scott from *The Office*. He didn't actually know that much about his team, but they knew way too much about him. The entrepreneur's role is to listen and to understand, not to overshare.

Find the place that feels authentic for you. And when you do interact with people, let them set the pace of sharing. One of your jobs is to respect their time so they can get the work done. Be brief and be gone, and remember that a little of you goes a long way.

CHOOSE WISELY

There's a saying that we are the average of the five or ten people we spend the most time with. As entrepreneurs, we have a lot of choice in selecting who those people are. Choosing your team well—inside and outside of your company—impacts your experience of work and can either encourage or weaken your commitment to compassionate leadership.

FIND YOUR PEERS

It really can be lonely at the top, especially as an entrepreneur. In big organizations, there are often lots of other people at, or at least near, your level. Executives at big companies have other executives to talk to and share their problems with. As entrepreneurs, we are in a different situation. You're the only one in your position.

Entrepreneurs also tend to devote an outsized portion of their lives to their companies. When our entire lives and communities lie inside the walls of our companies, it's harder not to get into friend territory with the people who work for us. That's why it's all the more important to have friends outside of work—or at least peers.

No matter what your specific company does, you can find peer groups of other entrepreneurs and business owners who are dealing with the same issues you're facing. At some level, all companies, and especially all small and entrepreneur-led companies, have essentially the same problems. The same organizational and financial concerns, the same challenges around people and communication and personalities, show up in every business.

Finding a peer group that shares these challenges will lighten your burden and reduce the loneliness of being the leader. It also reduces the desire to find friends or people to complain to, inside your company, and is a huge resource to draw on.

KNOW WHEN IT'S NOT A FIT

If you don't like firing people, congratulations. You're not an asshole. If we are not willing to fire people who aren't a fit for our companies, though, we're doing ourselves and everyone else in the company, including the person we don't want to fire, a disservice.

A couple of years ago, we had someone in the company who was making everyone miserable. Their entire attitude could be summed up in one phrase: "That's not my job." In a big company, they might get away with that attitude, but in a company of a few dozen people, it's visible to everyone. It's like they have a spotlight on them, and it affects the morale of the entire business. Every day, this person came in miserable, and that made everyone around them miserable.

I'm embarrassed to tell you how long I waited to fire this person. Every single other person in the company knew they needed to go, and I sat on it because I didn't want to be the bad guy. When I finally got the courage to do it, though, I learned my lesson immediately because the environment in the business changed *overnight*. The relief was incredible. People were suddenly able to have fun again, to enjoy their work. It blew me away how much effect one miserable person could have on everyone else.

And there's no question that this employee was miserable. It wasn't just that they weren't doing the job I needed them to do. They were unhappy because they weren't a good fit, and they knew it, and I knew, and they knew I knew it. That is not a happy place to be. If someone is miserable in my organization, that's not good for me, but it's also not good for them. It's not kind, or even nice, to them or anyone else, to keep making them show up every day. We're fooling ourselves into thinking we're helping them by refusing to do what everyone knows needs to be done.

This is the essence of compassion: making the tough decision that's for the greater good of the company and the individual. Of course, it might not seem like that in the moment. They're not going to thank you for firing them. They're going to be upset, and that's the part that you, as the leader, have to live with. Even when people are truly miserable, they also tend to be change-averse, and until they're forced to find something new, they won't go out and do it.

The question is, how do we know the difference between someone who needs compassion because they're going through a rough time, but they're going to go back to being a great employee when they get through it, and someone who is unhappy because they're not a fit?

When someone's not a fit for your organization, or your values, or your team, that is a persistent problem. It's always the same. Typically they will resist sharing personally (although not always), and won't bring you personal issues or ask for help. Professionally, they rarely ask any productive questions or bring up any ideas to help serve the greater good of the organization. Someone who needs your help, and deserves it, is a good employee who shows they care and does good work, and then suddenly slips, or has problems they didn't have before. When you go to them and ask what's going on, they recognize that they're slipping and take responsibility for it, and they will usually tell you (if you've earned their trust) what is causing the problem.

With that person, we should be happy to underwrite them and support them because there has been mutual caring and trust in the past. We know the performance will come back once the problem is dealt with. With the person who's not a fit, the performance was never there in the first place.

Maybe the biggest difference between the "not a fit" person and the good team member who is having a short-term issue is that the good team member will appreciate your help. The "not a fit" person will never appreciate you helping them, no matter how often you do it. You'll find yourself sinking more and more energy into helping them out and getting nothing, or even resentment, in return.

That's not the kind of person I want to spend time around, and I don't want to make my team spend their time around them, either.

THE HARD THING ABOUT THE RIGHT THING

There's a saying in the military that "the hard thing about the right thing is that it's the hard thing." Often, taking the actions that serve the greater good of your life, your team, and your community can seem like the hard thing. Fortunately, it's only hard in the short term.

If I were the kind of person to give in to that behavior, that would be the same as condoning it. I would be saying, "This is how the company operates: it's every man for himself, and get what you can." Construction is a small community. Word would get around. We would attract the worst kind of people, and it would become a miserable, self-centered, toxic experience. There would have been massive financial implications for my business, of course, but even more importantly, it would have radically altered the culture we've worked so hard to build.

It can seem easier to just give in when you're confronted with a difficult decision or a potential conflict. The key for me was long-term thinking. "What do I want in my life? Is this what I want in ten years? What kind of environment do I want to foster in my company? What do I want it to feel like when I go to work?"

Standing up for myself and not giving in to extortion showed the rest of the team what my values really were, not just what I said or what I wrote on the letterhead. It demonstrated, more than any number of meetings or even bonuses or incentive plans, what the company really stood for and what kind of culture we were creating. I was telling everyone and the universe, "This is a special culture, and I'm willing to tolerate short-term pain for myself to make sure we find the right people. I'm not going to tolerate people who aren't a good fit, or people who are selfish and put themselves above the greater good of the organization and everyone else in it."

A decision like that has a ripple effect. It told my leadership team what kind of people they should be looking for and hiring. It told my team that I wouldn't let any individual, no matter how important or senior, put themself about the good of the team. Making that decision was a form of honor and self-respect that everyone in the company can see.

Culture grows out of every single decision we make. Gritting our teeth and making the tough call in the moment can seem hard, but it will make our lives easier, and our companies better, long after that pain is over.

PUT IN THE TIME

Most of the time, the issue isn't that we don't know what to do. Most of us already know what the right thing to do is. Our guts tell us when we're acting in line with what we really value, and when we're taking the easy path or behaving in ways that aren't caring toward others.

The issue is that being authentic and compassionate and working toward the greater good gets forgotten, put aside, or not prioritized. We tell ourselves that we'll do that work once we're more profitable or when revenue is up, when it's actually the best way to get those outcomes.

Becoming the leader who can make tough but compassionate decisions takes work. Do the exercises in this book. Take the time to be self-reflective. Even when we already know, in our gut, what the right thing is, we need to give ourselves time to be aware of it and choose how to act on it.

MORE THAN FRIENDS

As the leader, we have the opportunity to give our team members something that they don't get from their friends: results.

It's like being on a sports team, seeing the progress you're making together and the wins you're achieving. Everyone on the team can get together and say, "Look what we did this year. We built this, we made this." No group of friends is going to get together and renovate a hospital, but our team does that every day. That's meaningful. Trying to be their friend doesn't just come across as tone deaf; it takes away the benefits and rewards they should be getting from working together with a leader.

As leaders, we can help people be accountable for achieving the things they want to achieve at work, and in their lives. We can help them feel valued, useful, and part of a bigger mission. Of all the things people say they want most in their lives, this is one of the most common: to be part of something bigger than themselves. You can give them that.

It should also be fun! Running a business well is a lot like a game with really high stakes. We are using our collective minds to solve problems and do things we could never do as individuals. Friendship is a social relationship. We have friendships for their own sake, and that is important. Leadership exists to achieve something. Without some result we're all trying to work toward together, there would be no point in having a leader.

And they know that as well as we do. They know we are not their friends. My team can see my name on their paycheck. I make decisions about their lives and judge their performance, and that's not a two-way street. That isn't a friendship. The trap is believing that makes it *less* than friendship: less important or less meaningful in their lives. Nothing could be further from the truth. If we let ourselves be leaders, if we can give them something to work toward and a caring, supportive culture to achieve it in, we'll be giving them something their friends can't.

At the end of our lives, we all want to remember our friends and families. As an entrepreneur, though, I bet you also want to remember your accomplishments: how you grew a business and created something out of nothing. True compassion is understanding that the people on your team are more like you than you might think. They want that, too.

Offering them the chance to do it with you is an incredible service to them, and it also happens to be the way to get the best possible results for your business.

You'll be especially glad you did that work when times get tough.

DISCOVERY EXERCISE: KIND OR NICE?

We're diving into the hard stuff here: are you being kind and compassionate to the people around you and to yourself, or are you being "nice" to avoid a hard conversation or a hard look at your own issues?

The line between "kind" and "nice" is complicated, and there are so many reasons we revert to being nice instead of being a leader. You might even need to talk to a coach or a therapist if you find yourself constantly avoiding making tough calls or needing people to like you so much that you don't do the leadership work that will build your business.

Find a time when you're not in a reactive state. Don't do this exercise when you're annoyed with someone or have just had a tough meeting. There's a saying that goes, "When your team is starting to annoy you, that's a great indicator that you might just need a vacation." If that's what you need, take it, and come back to this exercise when you're ready.

When you are calm, ask yourself, **Are there people you are being overly friendly with, or are there situations where you find yourself being "the nice guy" instead of taking the lead?**

Are you holding on to people who are not a fit because you don't want the short-term pain of confronting them? Is that keeping you from finding someone who would be truly great in that role? What about clients? If you have a bunch of clients that aren't a good fit for your business or your values, that's not just painful for you. It's making your entire team less effective for the great fit clients out there looking for you.

Think through *why* you are avoiding hard conversations or tough choices. You may have to work through the scarcity mindset or other underlying issues before you can shift this one. But trust me, the hard part is over quickly, whereas the benefits compound themselves for the long term.

8

WHEN COMPASSION GETS TOUGH

When COVID-19 hit, my company was hit hard. We'd had a good year in 2019, and the business was doing well, so we had planned to give substantial bonuses. Then COVID-19 happened, and suddenly I had to ask myself, "Do we still pay these? Or do we sit on the cash, just in case?" Paying out bonuses seemed irresponsible or even reckless, given the scary times.

It was not an easy decision. I run a construction company. We're not in tech or marketing. We couldn't just switch everyone online and keep moving. I had team members in their fifties and sixties who had never heard of Zoom, trying to figure out how to even show up to meetings.

We were also losing business. Construction was considered essential, and we do a lot of medical and hospital projects, so we did go back to work earlier than some people. But a lot of the jobs closed anyway. Clients were calling us and pulling their contracts, claiming *"force majeure"* (if you are an entrepreneur reading this book, you probably know what that means).

Even as an essential business, the work we had wasn't enough to keep the lights on.

At the same time, I was watching my wife go to work every day as an ICU nurse, all the way up through 2022. She did the whole tour. We were scared about the business failing, scared about losing our livelihood, and scared about her exposure to this new and largely unknown disease. There were a lot of reasons to scale back and hold on to as much money as possible.

That's the decision a lot of us entrepreneurs made at the time. I remember being in an entrepreneur group, sitting at home in our pajama bottoms on Zoom, trying to figure out what the hell was going on. Everybody was freaked out, saying, "We're not doing too great." No company does well when nobody is spending money: the entire world was suddenly in scarcity mode.

Later on, there were loans to help us get through it, but at that time, right at the beginning, nobody was even talking about that possibility.

On the call, many of my peers were saying, "We're not giving out bonuses. We can't afford it. We've got to save the money we have." I'm not blaming them by any means. Each of us has to figure out for ourselves and our own businesses what we can afford. And if we don't take care of our companies, they won't exist long enough to take care of us and our teams.

All of that being true, I decided to go ahead and give out the bonuses anyway. My feeling was, my team worked hard. They earned these bonuses. They're the ones who gave us a successful year last year and, if we all survive COVID-19, they're the ones who will create success for the company in the future. And they didn't just earn that money—they needed it. They were struggling and scared and trying to support their families, too.

Even though no one said it out loud, they were all looking to me and asking, "How is this company going to take care of me now that things are tough?"

I made the decision, and I said, "These are scary times, but we're not going anywhere. We're resilient. I'm committed to this company, and I'm committed to you, so here is the bonus that you earned."

Talking to my peers in the entrepreneur's group, I could tell they thought I was nuts. Most of them weren't giving bonuses. They were going the other way, laying people off and reducing costs. My company has never laid anyone off—that's part of our investment in our team—and I wasn't going to be the one to start, even in what anybody would agree was an exceptional circumstance.

It's been five years, and I still don't regret that decision. Things are different after COVID-19. Business is harder. It's harder to make a good profit. But when I look around, I see that my own company, and my clients that have adopted the compassionate mindset, are the ones that have made it through and stayed strong.

One thing I can say for sure is that the people on my team who got bonuses during COVID-19 are more invested in the company's success than they have ever been. They knew what other companies were doing. They had friends and neighbors getting laid off or not getting bonuses. They understood that what we did was unusual.

They also understood something that I learned in the military: we are what we do when times are tough. The way we act whenever everything is going exactly the way we want doesn't say much about our character. Character shows when life gets hard.

But you can't wait for hard times and see how you respond.

The commitment to being compassionate in a storm is to practice when the sun is shining.

OVERDRAWING THE ACCOUNT

Even if you've never served in the military, you've probably seen movies or TV shows about military training. The movie version isn't exactly like reality, but one thing about it is accurate: military training is designed to prepare you for the worst conditions possible. If we had only trained for best-case scenarios, we would not have been prepared for the actual conditions of combat. When you train for the worst, and then the conditions you meet aren't quite that bad, it actually seems kind of easy, strangely enough.

At the same time, military training isn't all suffering. There are moments of bonding and camaraderie, even in the worst situations. That can happen, in part, because you've done the work to shore up relationships during the good times, when people are relaxed and not under stress.

There's a concept from the book *The Five Love Languages* called "deposits and withdrawals." Leadership relies on relationships, and compassion is based on love, so these concepts can offer insight into how leadership relationships work, too.

In every relationship, you have a kind of account with the person, and you're constantly putting in deposits and taking out withdrawals. Deposits are things like offering them support, helping them out, listening, and caring about them. In a business relationship, deposits are sometimes actual cash investments, like raises and bonuses, but deposits also include all the compassionate and caring work you are hopefully doing with your team. Withdrawals happen when you need something from them. As a leader, you make withdrawals when you ask someone to work overtime, or when you ask for commitment from them in tough times.

We need to make deposits when times are good because when things get rough, we will be making withdrawals. If we haven't put in the effort to be caring and compassionate, to invest in people, and to build our culture, then when downturns like COVID-19 come along, we'll be overdrawing—trying to take out something that we never put in in the first place.

On the other hand, if we do the right thing when it's hard, like giving bonuses in a tight year, that creates exponentially more loyalty. We get more credit in the account for the same level of investment.

Like everything else in this book, this isn't something I'm perfect at. A few months into COVID-19, we had the opportunity to apply for loans to help us make it through. One of the leaders on my team was in charge of the applications, and he forgot to apply to one completely. We did receive money from government grants to get us through COVID-19, but not nearly as much as we should have.

That's when I lost it. At that point, I was under an enormous amount of stress, and I was in a scarcity mindset because we'd left money on the table. I laid into him. I took it out on him so hard, in fact, that he ended up quitting soon after.

That was too big of a withdrawal to make from him, especially at that moment. There wasn't enough credit to get past it.

The expectation of a leader is that we're the ones to up our game and find a way, even in the hardest times. If we don't, we won't have a company. At that moment, everyone on Earth was worried about the planet, worried about their families, worried about the economy—and on top of that, I had to be thinking about the business and its future. My company has been around for nearly 40 years. My dad built it and nurtured it. All I could think was, *Am I going to be the one to tank this thing?*

We needed the money, not just for me or for the survival of my dad's business, but for all the other families we were supporting. His mistake was critical. On the other hand, by the time I yelled at him, it was too late to change what had happened. Since then, I've come to sincerely regret the way I reacted. Imagine someone being so angry at you that they want to quit and never work with you again. It was clearly not my finest hour. But I learned a valuable lesson to make deposits in the good times. That includes deposits I make in myself, like meditating, so that I have the capacity to be compassionate when things go wrong.

The hard part of being an entrepreneur, especially in tough times, is that business moves fast, and we don't always know the right answer. Even with all the preparation we've done in the rest of the book—self-reflection, investing in people, developing trust, and everything else—we will still make mistakes, or take actions we aren't sure are the right ones.

We do the best we can, and sometimes that means trying something, even if you don't know whether it will work. Sometimes the wrong decision is better than no decision. In the end, our job as entrepreneurs is to ensure that we're learning from both the bad and good decisions so that we can improve.

TIED TO THE SHIP

The entrepreneur and their business are bound together. Until they sell it, the business is tied to them, their decisions, and their character. Whatever we are, our businesses will reflect that, and however the business does, that's how our lives will go.

If my business fails, I will definitely fail. The captain goes down with the ship. It's a *fait accompli*.

Employees aren't tied to the company in the same way. They can jump ship when things get tough. The question is how to create a culture where the ones you want to stay don't want to leave.

Ultimately, it's not good for anybody to jump ship all the time. We have all seen the resumes of people who leap to a new position every six months for a couple grand more a year, and I can see that they pretty quickly price themselves out of a job.

I had someone like that on my team a few years ago. We were training him to have a larger role in the organization with increased responsibilities. He came to me and told me he'd had another offer that would pay 20 percent more per hour and wanted to know if I'd match it, or if he should leave.

I asked him if they had benefits as good as ours. I told him, "Look, construction is a feast-and-famine business. They got a big job and hired a bunch of people, but they're going to lay off most of them as soon as the job is done. You know we don't do layoffs. We're committed to keeping you on. But you do what you need to do."

He took the job. A month later, he called me and said, "I don't have any benefits, I don't have job security, I think they're going to lay people off. This company doesn't have a long-term plan for me, they don't have projects coming in, and I'm the most recent hire. Will you take me back?"

By that point I'd already filled the position. There's a personality profile of thinking the next thing is going to be the best, and that generally doesn't fit our culture. Trust and investment go both ways.

I have a buddy like that. He's single, and he's on all the dating apps. He'll meet a woman, go out a few times, and then start going out with another one. He can't settle down because he's always thinking about the next one. He can't just be with the person he's with and enjoy that time. That's the culture we're in: there are infinite movies to watch, infinite people you can meet, infinite food you could have delivered, infinite options.

At this point, my wife and I have a rule. After the kids go to bed, if we're going to watch a movie, we pick something, and we just watch it. We made that rule after we found ourselves spending so much time picking something that we'd realize we could have watched a whole movie by the time we picked something.

As an entrepreneur, I have to fight that, too. It's not just employees who get pulled into that mindset. Being tied to the ship means it's hard for an entrepreneur to decide to get another job, but it also means that whatever wild goose chase I decide to go on, the business is going with me.

I'm just recently learning to graduate from the mindset of constantly chasing the next thing, and focus instead on what kind of person I'm becoming—because whatever kind of person I am, that's the kind of business and culture I'm going to have. If the first thing I do in my day is go out and chase new stuff, and the very last thing I do (if I have time) is meditate or self-reflect, then I'm going to create a culture where everyone else is doing the same. They'll be chasing new opportunities, looking for something else all the time. I still have a lot of work to do on this, but I recognize it more when it's happening.

The benefits go both ways, too, though. If I live in the mindset of being happy with what I have and committing to the people around me, the culture of my business will be better, and people will want to stay. Since I'm the one tied to the ship, I'm the one who benefits most from that. My team members can come and go if that's what they choose, but I'm stuck with this thing I built. For my own sake, I want to make it a place people want to stay, since one of those people is me.

Like all the other elements of building your business, that work starts when times are good.

REFOCUSING ON THE PEOPLE WHO MATTER MOST

I can remember one moment in particular when my attitude shifted.

I'd had a hard day at work, and I walked in the door and saw my wife and kids, and I had a sudden thought: *Wow, I get to be with these amazing human beings!*

It was a much bigger feeling than just not taking them for granted, or being grateful for them. It was amazement that these amazing human beings were part of my life, and that I got to spend time around them.

Much too often, the people I love the most are the ones I've taken most for granted. In the back of my mind was this thought, like, *Oh, they'll always be there.* The people we care about most almost become background in our lives. We're chasing the new client, building the business, or whatever, and we forget that these people we love are right here in front of us.

My brother's death was a wake-up call. I took our time together for granted because I didn't know how much, or rather how little, time we had left. I didn't want that to happen with any of the other important people in my life.

Shifting that mindset is where it all starts. You cannot be authentically compassionate with your team at work until you're compassionate with your loved ones at home. Look around you at the people you share your life with, and share your gratitude for them in the everyday moments when everything is going fine. Don't wait until tragedy strikes or you're in a family crisis to show them their importance.

The same thing applies professionally. All of the exercises

in the book, everything I've laid out, are so much easier when you're not in crisis mode. Practice compassion and caring when you're having an easy, low-stakes conversation, not when someone is talking about leaving the company. Practice being present and curious about day-to-day stuff, because it's really hard to nail that out of the gate when someone is screaming in your face.

I learned in the Army that when things get tough, you revert to the *worst* of your training, the lowest level. When COVID-19 hits, or you're in an argument with someone, you're not suddenly going to develop all the compassion skills you need to handle it well.

You get to spend time with these people all the time. That's a gift even when it just seems like a humdrum day, or nothing important is happening. Use it.

THE GIFT OF THE UNEXPECTED

My wife and I met on a blind date. That's not all that unusual—but the way we ended up on that date was wildly unexpected.

Back in high school, I was on the wrestling team. I had an archrival, a wrestler at another school that we competed against a lot, and he and I ended up wrestling each other in the state championships twice.

The first year we wrestled each other in the state championships, I won. The next year, he won. We were both serious about wrestling, and we did not like each other. In the end, I pushed myself to get my weight down so I wouldn't be competing in the same weight class as him. That's how much I didn't want to lose to him again.

Fast forward ten years. I'm at the gym, and I see someone who looks familiar, and of course, it turns out to be my old rival. At this point, I'm not sixteen anymore, so I say hi, and we end up becoming friends. He started dating a girl, and while he was dating her, he was over at her apartment, and he met her roommate. He thought I might like her, so he set us up on a blind date.

We've been married fourteen years—and the arch rival who introduced us is now my financial advisor.

This is a story about compassion because it would have been very easy for me to turn around and ignore him. Even as an adult, years after our last interaction, it was hard to get over my initial feeling that this was a person I didn't like, who had been my rival.

If you can't control the unexpected—by definition—you also can't predict the positive, sometimes life-changing benefits that can come from it. Even though the outcomes of this encounter were positive, it teaches the same lesson as leading during COVID-19: compassion is always good preparation. Kindness, forgiveness, seeing the other person's perspective, and caring about people even when it's hard will always bring positive things back to you, even if sometimes you don't see the results for more than a decade.

Often, the results are a lot more immediate. A few years ago, we were working on a project, and I was having a hard time with the owner's rep. Their mindset was, "Don't make me look bad, and don't surprise me." In renovation work, that's almost impossible. There are always surprises.

For weeks, it felt like we were struggling to communicate and that everything was an emergency. It seemed like the client wanted updates almost hourly all day long. It was frustrating.

But then I stepped back and got curious. I asked myself, *Why isn't this working?*

I realized that this client's superiors didn't understand much about construction or the renovation process, so the client was getting pressure to get constant updates from me. What they needed wasn't a lot of detailed descriptions of the work. They needed short, bullet-point updates to keep their superiors in the loop and communicate the overall project status.

Instead of trying to force the client to do things the way I was used to, I looked at the situation from their perspective and changed the way I communicated. Instead of the long engineering and construction explanations I'd been sending, I started emailing three or four bullet points: *here's what is happening, here's why it's happening, here's what we are doing about it, and here's what you can expect.*

I'd actually been giving that client too much information because the focus was on me: demonstrating that my team and I were doing the right thing and keeping the project on track. Flipping my mindset to see the client's needs showed me that I needed to ask first, not tell.

I'm almost ashamed to admit how many times I had to learn this lesson before it started to stick. When I first started as a business coach, I came in with that same arrogance. I approached it with a feeling that I knew the material like the back of my hand, and my whole demeanor was basically, "Listen up while I explain this to you."

In one session, I spent almost an hour explaining to my client what he needed to do, and then, when our time was almost up, he asked a question that made me realize I hadn't understood his situation at all, and I'd just wasted both of our time giving him a lot of information that was not going to be relevant. If I had just asked him a few questions, instead of jumping in with my supposed expertise, we would have accomplished a lot more.

A powerful transition happens when we switch from having the right answer to asking questions and letting the other person find the answer. When we realize that it's actually their journey, not ours, we can step back and let them figure out what they need. In fact, we come to realize that only they can possibly know the right answer for their own problem—and everyone learns more in the process.

The difference I saw between the businesses that weathered COVID-19 and came back strong, and the ones that struggled or even went under, was exactly this difference in mindset. If an entrepreneur went into COVID-19 thinking that they were the only one in the company who could solve problems, the only one with the answers, they were not as flexible or adaptable when the unexpected happened. No one is going to solve something as complex and unprecedented as COVID-19 on their own, and if I, as the entrepreneur, think I'm the only one with the answers, I only have access to my own, limited expertise.

When we step back, look from the other person's perspective, and encourage everyone around us to do their own thinking, the results are less predictable. That can feel scary to those of us who like to control every little thing. But it also creates the potential for ideas, benefits, and outcomes that you would never have imagined or thought of on your own. In almost every case, it means a lot less work for you, too. Sometimes it might even change the course of your whole life. Just ask my wife.

EVERYONE IS SMARTER THAN ME

I'm not saying that every individual on Earth is smarter than I am. Entrepreneurs tend to be smart, capable people, and I have confidence that I know what I'm doing. But there's no way I can ever be as smart as *everyone*.

My entire team, taken altogether, is more capable and has more expertise and more ideas than just me alone. Building that team when things are good, when I have the capacity and the resources to find and train people, sets me up to have the team I need in the hard times.

In fact, a good team can keep an entrepreneur from creating self-inflicted hard times.

I'm not perfect. I don't always make the right decision. If the company is tied to me and my choices, that means if I make a dumb business decision, I can single-handedly create hard times for the business. A good team can prevent you from making those mistakes.

Entrepreneurs in particular are prone to wanting to do everything. We chase the next thing, and we want all the stuff. The problem is, we can't be profitable at all of it, and not all of it belongs in the business.

I'm in construction, so when I saw people flipping houses by throwing in a new floor and a fresh coat of paint and selling the home for a massive profit, I thought, *I can do that*. I also had skilled labor available inside my company. COVID-19 had slowed down our new projects, and I had teams ready and waiting who could do the work on these houses in no time.

It seemed like easy money, so I bought a house and started planning the remodel. The problem is, I'm a contractor. I wanted everything to be top quality. I couldn't just slap on a coat of paint and call it a day. I was putting way too much money into the house and cutting into my profit. In my entrepreneurial brain, I thought all that "free" labor was going to make the flips more profitable.

I ended up putting a lot of time, money, and energy into that project and not making a lot of profit. Fortunately, I had the sense to recognize what was happening, and I only ended up flipping one house.

I had been a leader for a long time, but I was still so sure

I had all the answers. Now, if I suggested that, my leadership team would sit me down and say, "No, let's focus on what we do," and they would be right. If I want to flip houses, I can start another company that does that, but it's not what we do in this business.

As entrepreneurs, we love new ideas, new projects, and the potential for additional revenue streams. That vision is generally positive for our companies. It's what drives new business and keeps the company growing. But pursuing every opportunity that comes up isn't in the interest of the business, and pulling the entire team along with me because I got a new idea wasn't compassionate. I was seeing my own goals and following my own desires without asking my leadership team's opinion or focusing on the greater good.

THE BEST MEETING EVER

I had a powerful reminder of this switch from telling to trusting when I lost my voice at an important industry conference. I could only say a few words at a time during the entire event, and I ended up listening a lot more.

When I got back, I sat in on a meeting with my team, and I still couldn't say more than a sentence or two—and it was one of the best meetings I've ever been in. The team brought up challenges and generated creative solutions, and I got to sit back and observe their brilliance. After a decade as an entrepreneur, I'd finally figured out what it looked like to scale: it meant me doing less. All that because I couldn't speak.

That experience started me thinking about how valuable it would be if words were a scarce resource. Think about how that would change our interactions. Imagine if every time we went into a meeting, we were only allowed four questions and two sentences. I know I would think very hard about what those sentences would be. I'd want to nail it every time I opened my mouth.

That kind of precision and focus is especially important because our teams are very much like our kids in that they listen to everything we say. The words we choose to use will stick with them and echo in their minds, for good or bad.

My tendency is to be over-prepared when I go into meetings. In the past, I've walked into meetings with so much to say that I jumped in and started saying it right away. As I've learned trust and compassion with my team, I have given up a lot of that, and I'm seeing the results. I just had a quarterly meeting with my leadership team, and I prepared zero. Nothing.

I let them run the meeting without me, and they nailed it. They worked through issues, figured out solutions, and got through everything on the agenda. I didn't add anything until the last few minutes, and that was mostly to tell them what an incredible job they were doing.

One of them came up to me afterward and said, "That was the best meeting we've ever had."

If I had listened to my ego, I could have left that conversation thinking, "I don't add any value" or "Next time, I need to take more control." After doing the self-reflection and self-compassion work, though, I was able to see the real point: I just got back hours and hours of time that I used to be spending preparing for work that other people are already doing.

When we get to that point, the stress of running a business drops by about 90%. I know for sure that if something as hard and complicated as COVID-19 happens again, my team will be able to handle it. Maybe I'll even be able to take a vacation—and for most entrepreneurs, that's a lot rarer than a crisis.

DO THE WORK BEFORE YOU NEED IT

Compassion offers us so many benefits as entrepreneurs. It helps us prepare for the unexpected, get through hard times, build our companies, retain employees, and grow our bottom line. In the end, though, compassion is about something much more important: it's about human beings caring for each other and themselves. Caring for others at that level isn't something that can be learned or made up in the moment. It requires us to be prepared ahead of time.

What happened to my brother in Iraq is an extreme example, but I think it's a powerful reminder of why you should start working on compassion now—even if you're not sure when or how you will need it.

My brother never told me this story. I heard it third-hand. My brother was deployed in Iraq, probably in 2007 or 2008, and his unit had to clear a cave system. My brother, according to the story I heard, went to his commander and said, "Sir, this is an empty cave system, and I'm concerned about the safety of these guys. Can we clear it with frag grenades so we don't risk anyone getting hurt?"

The commander refused. He told my brother that the cave system needed to be cleared.

My brother told him, "I'm not going to send my guys in. If someone has to go in, I'll go."

He was barely inside when the entire cave system collapsed on him. It took several hours to get him out after it collapsed, and they had to use dogs to find him in the rubble. Part of me thinks he never really left that cave. Or that he left a part of himself there.

My brother showed an incredible level of empathy and courage in that moment. If you're willing to go into the cave for your team, they will make it happen for you, whatever you ask of them.

When he got back home, he began to distance and isolate himself from everyone he knew. He stopped going to the doctor or the dentist. He totally stopped taking care of himself a long time before he died. He didn't know how to get what he needed. The negative stigma around mental health in our culture is almost as bad as in the military. When I was in the infantry, when one of the soldiers had to go to the therapist, the leaders called it "going to see the wizard," and everybody knew what that meant.

The negative stigma my brother encountered in the military followed him into his civilian life, making it even more difficult for him to get help.

There was no opportunity and no help for my brother to prepare for the emotional toll ahead of time, or have compassion for himself after it happened. He struggled with mental health issues his entire life, and his work as a lawyer, keeping people from being involuntarily committed, contributed as well.

It's impossible to know what might have helped him, or whether his death might have been preventable. What I do know is that we will all, at some point in our lives, be confronted with difficult situations that require compassion for ourselves and others. A worldwide pandemic, where no one is allowed to leave the house for months, would have seemed like an unthinkable scenario just a few years ago.

We can't prepare for or prevent every situation we're going to encounter. What we can and must do is develop the self-awareness, self-care, and compassion we will need when it does.

Part of my work in this book is to make the work of compassion—for others and for yourself—less of a stigma. I see a therapist. I talk about these issues with my leadership team. You never know what people are going through, or what crisis might be right around the next corner.

I wasn't doing this kind of work prior to COVID-19, at least not anywhere near the level I'm doing now. I was taking care of myself physically, but not paying attention to my own mental health. What saved me, and saved the company, was the habit my dad started, and that I followed, of taking care of the team first. Whether that was giving out bonuses, letting them take a truck to care for a sick family member, or just listening, the blueprint of compassion was there. Everything I've done since then has built on that and strengthened it.

As leaders, it's our job to do that work for ourselves, for our team, and for our company. You don't sharpen the steel when you're in a swordfight, and you don't clean your weapon in the middle of a gunfight. My hope here is that the painful, difficult lessons I've learned about caring can help you take that journey before circumstances force you to.

In the end, the lesson is simple. When you're alone, even if you're surrounded by people, things are scary. Every crisis seems insurmountable. When you've got twenty or fifty or however many people who are on your team—who trust you, and who you genuinely care about—you can accomplish a lot more. I see this when two veterans with PTSD get together and talk. All of a sudden, they're not alone anymore.

As scary as COVID-19 was, I was never as scared as a lot of entrepreneurs and business owners I knew because I had this group of invested people who I trusted to take care of me, and to take care of the business. My father's legacy of compassion paved the way for that, and my journey to understand and build caring into the company culture has taken us even farther.

Take a few first steps and see how it feels. When you look back on what you've done, I can promise that the work you did to show compassion to the people around you won't be the part you regret.

DISCOVERY EXERCISE: DO THEY WANT TO STAY?

COVID-19 broke a lot of companies, and in my experience, the companies that broke fastest and didn't come back were the ones that missed the ball on compassion. If you weren't taking care of your people before COVID-19, they were that much more likely to jump ship as soon as things got tough. Employee costs skyrocketed during COVID-19 because people kept bouncing around, looking for a little more money. Even now that the world is basically back to normal, there's still a sense of higher turnover and less loyalty.

People who are treated well don't think that way. They don't constantly look around for a job that might give them a couple thousand extra dollars. In particular, the people who are cared for during tough times are the most likely to stay where they are.

So ask yourself, honestly: What is your turnover like? If one of the key members of your team got an offer somewhere else, would they tell you—or would they just leave?

This is more than just a question about turnover. In a sense, it's a bellwether for your entire business and a one-shot assessment of your compassion as a leader. People who are treated well and cared for might still leave if they get an unbelievable opportunity (like working on the beach with their children), but they're not going to jump around for a raise, or because your business has a tougher year.

CONCLUSION

My brother's death was earth-shattering for me. It was so incredibly hard. Like most hard things, there were a lot of valuable lessons that came out of it, and I didn't want those lessons to go to waste. That's why I wrote this book.

Before my brother died, suicide wasn't something I ever thought about. I certainly didn't see suicide prevention as part of my job as a leader in my business. As entrepreneurs, we have so much to deal with already. We're often overwhelmed and putting in eighty- or ninety-hour weeks. It can be hard to hear that we need to add compassion on top of that, or that our behavior might have a profound impact on the mental health of someone who works for us.

My brother's death brought home to me that I don't have a choice. As a leader, I work with people, not just machines or operating systems. And people sometimes need help that goes beyond helping them do their job. Statistically, if you're a leader, the likelihood is that you're working with someone right now who is struggling with suicidal thoughts, or is wrestling with related mental health issues. When leaders are compassionate, they are less likely to burn out. Their employees are less likely to suffer in silence. Their families are more supported, and their communities become safer and healthier.

The math is staggering. If this book reaches one million leaders, who touch the lives of an average of two hundred people each, that's a total of two hundred million people. If we could reduce suicide risk among those two hundred million people by just 25 percent, that would mean fifty thousand lives. If we could reduce the risk by 50 percent, it would be one hundred thousand lives.

That's why my goal is to help build one million compassionate companies by 2035. Not soft companies, or slow companies. Companies led by entrepreneurs who take care of themselves and create cultures that take care of others.

MY BROTHER'S LEGACY

Since his suicide, I've had a lot of hard memories of my brother. I wish I could say we had a better relationship. I wish I could say I don't have any regrets. I wish I could say I remember him fondly. We had so many fights, and at the time, they seemed to come out of nowhere. In hindsight, I can see that he was struggling, but at the time, I thought he was blaming me.

We all do this. We overemphasize our role in other people's lives. In reality, those tense moments and arguments are the other person showing us a mirror of their own issues. I think I was angry with my brother for a lot of my life, and I'm ashamed to say that I couldn't see that he was struggling. I thought we just had a bad relationship. We did—but his struggles were also showing themselves, and I didn't see them.

Just before he died, my brother sent me an email. He wouldn't get on the phone with me no matter how many times I called, but he wrote to me. The email was all about how things weren't going the way he wanted them to—however since my dad died, nothing was the same.

I wrote back and told him, basically, "Well, what do you have control over? What can you do to make things better?" I handed him a lot of advice (in the form of a question, but still advice) about how to get a grip on his life.

That led to his last email, and the last words I would ever get from him. Except for the more pleasant voicemails I've saved from him, his last words were not kind.

He died that same day.

I was in a meeting when I got the text about his death. When I got in contact with the police department in Seattle, I was put in touch with the officer who was the first responder on the scene. He was a veteran, and it turned out we had served in Iraq at the same time. It was incredibly touching and meaningful to have a fellow veteran be the one to tell me about how my brother died, even though the details were not pleasant. My brother was a vet, too, so it felt like the three of us shared a bond.

I also requested that the police department send me all the information they had about the death. If I had it to do over again, I wouldn't make that request. The photos of my brother's suicide are burned into my mind forever. He died by firearm. Firearms are the number one cause of suicides, and the vast majority of firearm deaths are suicides. This isn't about gun control or getting on a pedestal; it's about saving lives. The more barriers we put between the people we love and access to a firearm, the less likely you will be to experience what I experienced. Double lock your safe. Keep the trigger guard locked. Keep your ammunition in a separate place.

I wrote earlier about the pain of telling my mother about my brother's death. I wouldn't wish that on anyone.

It wasn't until later that I understood how condescending my response to him had been. He was struggling, and he reached out to me in the only way he knew how. He was the kind of person who wouldn't take help. He worked as an attorney, and his job was to prevent people with mental health issues from being institutionalized, so even when he went to the VA for support for his own mental illness and suicidal ideations, he knew exactly what to say so that they could not hold him against his will. That was a kind of last try for him, to reach out for help—but not really reach out for help by avoiding being held there.

I am ashamed, too, that I was annoyed at hearing him complain again and annoyed, as only an older brother can be annoyed, that he seemed like he wouldn't get his act together. So instead of hearing that he needed me, I talked down to him. I gave him advice he didn't want and acted like I knew how he should live his life and what he was doing wrong.

I couldn't see that he was asking for my help because the way he asked for it stirred up all of our history and all of my reactivity. I'd been in the military, too. I had also lost our dad, and I was getting on with it, so from on high, I explained things to him instead of listening. Hearing about his problems over email didn't help, either. It's almost impossible to tell someone's mood or feelings in an email. That's why I prefer the phone for important conversations.

I definitely didn't see that I also needed support and therapy and help understanding my own feelings. The pain and sorrow I felt, the mourning I went through, were devastating. I struggled especially with the "why." I asked myself, over and over, whether I could have done anything to change what happened. The seven stages of grief aren't linear. I was all over the place—from anger to denial, to blame, and back again.

It took nearly two years to get to a place where his death could mean something more than that pain and grief.

When he first died, I called the integrator at my company, and told him, "I don't know if I'll come back to work." That's how hard it hit me.

Finally, I began to think more clearly about how I wanted to remember his life. I needed a way to make his death meaningful. I thought about starting something totally new, like a suicide prevention nonprofit. But the more I thought about it, the more I realized that it would be most impactful to change the way I did what I was already doing.

Genuinely caring about the people who were already around me—that would be even more impactful than starting something new. I cannot underscore enough how much difference it makes to authentically care, and let people know that you care. You don't have to be perfect at it. You just have to try.

I don't know whether that kind of genuine caring would have changed things for my brother. I would like to think that, if he'd had this kind of compassion in his professional life, he might still be here, but one of the things I had to learn after he died was that people who are well don't die by suicide. You just can't ever know what would or would not have made a difference, or if anything would.

That doesn't change, for me, how important this is.

Since his death, I've become more present. I take a lot less for granted, especially the people around me. And that's what has led me to compassion as a person and as a leader. We need more of this in the world, and in our companies. Statistically, if you have even a few people working for you, the unfortunate likelihood is that at least one of them is struggling in some way.

My hope is that, if they knew their boss or leader really cared about them, it might make a tiny difference. That's all I want. That's how my brother's life, and death, have changed me: I understand now that struggling isn't something people wear on their sleeves. Suicide is a hidden illness, and because of the stigma around mental health in our society, it hides itself even more.

They say that solitary confinement is one of the most severe punishments you can inflict on a person because it takes away their social interactions. People who are struggling with suicide move away from social interactions, and like my brother, they find themselves more and more alone. If we can make even some of those interactions more positive and caring, maybe we can reduce some of that pain, and maybe even reduce suicide. That's why all the profits from this book are going to suicide prevention, and that's why I wrote the book in the first place: to share this vitally important lesson so that you don't have to learn it the way I did.

My brother was a hard person to understand. He could be the life of the party, even when he was at his lowest point. It's hard for me to know how I felt about him and his death, and what I could have done about it. Part of me thinks that I never knew how bad it was or that he was considering suicide, but another part of me thinks I knew all along. There's a feeling—and I know because I used to have it, too—that if someone needs help, they'll say something. So we give advice or tell people, "just do your job," with no idea that these other struggles might be going on underneath.

Or you might tell yourself, "No one in my company is struggling. This doesn't apply to me," or "If someone's going to die by suicide, there's nothing you can do." My response to that is, if you have a bunch of people in your life who know you really care about them, where is the downside?

The fact that you'll get better business results is a nice bonus.

The real value will be in how people feel when they're around you, and how you feel every day around them. That's why I talk with my leadership team about these issues. I don't share my personal issues or expect them to talk through trauma with me. That's why I have a therapist. I give myself the compassion of having a support team, and there are things I discuss with my therapist, things I discuss with my business coach, and things I bring up with my leadership team. It wouldn't be caring to them to make them deal with my personal issues—and it's not compassionate to make your team deal with your unconscious, undealt-with issues because you can't give yourself that support.

My greatest hope for this book is to make it acceptable to be compassionate as a leader, to create the caring and trust that would allow someone to speak up and say, "I'm having a problem, and I need some help." My brother never did that with me. He had the mindset we both learned in the military, to just "shut the fuck up and keep going."

As entrepreneurs, we can fall into that same way of thinking. I hope that what I have shared in this book encourages you to shift that mindset and gives you tools to start being compassionate with your family, with your team, and with yourself.

IT'S NOT ABOUT ADVICE

The email before he died wasn't the first time I gave my brother advice he didn't listen to.

When we were younger, it seemed like he was always complaining about things or talking about how his life wasn't going the way he wanted. I gave him what seemed like good ideas, and yet again, he didn't do any of the things I suggested, and I decided I'd had enough. I told him, "Don't bring me your problems if you're not going to take my advice."

Looking back, it sounds like something a twenty-two-year-old would say—someone who was sure he had all the answers. Unfortunately, we as leaders can take the same approach to people on our team, basically telling them, "Don't say anything to me unless you're going to do what I tell you." The ultimate dismissive phrase a leader can use is, "Don't bring me a problem without a solution." It's our job as leaders to ask the right questions to help the person develop a solution.

Developing compassion has led me to radically shift my approach. Our job isn't to have all the answers, but to work ourselves out of a job so we can do the stuff we're really good at, that only we can do. I don't need to be the only person who can make decisions in order to be valuable to my business.

I have one coaching client who told me, "I want to be the last person to see everything that goes out. I should be making the final call on everything." He was also a veteran, so I asked him, "Hey, do you remember in the Army ever having a commander who insisted on overseeing every little thing you did?"

He stared at me and said, "Oh my god. I'm that guy." He suddenly saw the role he was playing and the effect it was having on his business. You cannot scale a business in which one person makes all the decisions. It just isn't possible.

Sometimes, even when you're absolutely sure you do have the right answer, you still have to let other people figure it out on their own. Just this morning, I was walking my dog, listening to meditative music, enjoying the beautiful weather. I was thinking about my brother, about saying goodbye, and about this book and how I wanted to end it, when a woman pulled up next to me in her car and asked for directions.

Honestly, I try to help others wherever I can, I'm pretty good at directions, and I didn't want to be a jerk. So I gave her precise directions, and she thanked me, thought about it for a moment, rolled up her window, and drove off in the exact opposite direction from where I'd told her to go. I said, "Go up to the next intersection and take a right," and she drove up to the intersection and immediately turned left.

For a moment, I was annoyed. Why bother asking for directions if you're not going to follow them? I was in the army for ten years, I'm really good at land navigation (thanks to army directions training), and I was walking around my own neighborhood, so I knew for a fact that I had the right answer.

But having the right answer doesn't mean the other person will listen. Ultimately, they have to figure out the answer for themselves. There's a story about my dad, when he was out in the field. He had a meeting with one of his field superintendents, who brought him an issue with the construction of the building. My dad asked him, "What are you going to do about it?" The superintendent gave a solution that didn't make any sense, and my dad said, "Sounds good," and walked away.

A bunch of us asked him, "Why didn't you tell him that wasn't going to work?"

He said, "Him doing his solution, his way is better than him doing my solution half-assed and not getting it done.

The person with the problem is the only one who can find a solution. The lady who needed directions has to figure out her issues with navigation on her own.

Compassion isn't just about asking how someone's weekend was or their kids' names. It's not about giving what you think are the best instructions and then expecting them to follow your notes exactly. You have to be a good coach, and that means finding out where they are going and helping them get there. Sometimes it means letting them find their own path, even if it looks to you like they're going in the wrong direction.

What's important is stopping the advice for a minute and listening. It's creating enough trust that they can come to you when they think they're getting off course, or if they are struggling. If they don't take the turns you think they should take, maybe they are showing you a new way to get there.

YOU CAN'T BE EVERYTHING TO EVERYONE

If it doesn't change the outcome of a situation, what's the point? What if you're kind and authentically caring to someone, and they still leave the company, or turn out to be a bad fit, or underperform?

My answer to that is: how do you know it didn't change the outcome? We don't live in the multiverse. You can't know how every single decision or action turns out. In the end, I believe that compassion does change the outcome, even if you can't see it. People who know they are cared for work together better than those who don't. They care more about themselves and each other. That changes the outcome. Maybe it doesn't always lead to higher revenue this quarter, but it does create loyalty, and trust, and commitment, and those have long-term effects that can only be beneficial.

The flip side of that coin is that you can't be everything to everyone. You can't change people who don't want to change, and compassion isn't a tactic to control specific outcomes.

Suicide survivors have to find a way to live with two difficult and contradictory truths. Suicide is preventable—and you couldn't have prevented your loved one's suicide. I think about this all the time. I know there were times when I could have been a better big brother. I know that my brother struggled with things that he never told me about, and that I could have done a better job listening. But I also know that there are people you can't help—not necessarily because they can't be helped, but because you are not the person who can help them.

My brother stopped picking up the phone when I called years before he died. He made it pretty clear that he didn't want me in his life. As hard as it is to accept, there are people who are just not interested in you, in your compassion, or in your personality. They don't want to see your face. It's not that they aren't worth the effort, but they aren't going to be able to accept that effort from you. Far from it. Some people will never accept even your very best efforts.

I've been thinking a lot recently about how life isn't like the movies. The differences in life are subtle. Like the other day, when I saw a mother and son who looked exactly alike. You would never see that in the movies. Something like that only happens in real life.

Grief is like that. It's strange and complicated, and it doesn't work the way it looks in the movies. It's not a straight line trajectory, and the answers aren't clear-cut. Accepting that people can be helped, and that maybe, at the same time, I couldn't help my brother, is like that. That kind of subtlety is too real and difficult for the movies.

I don't want the discoveries I've made about this to belong just to me. I honestly did not understand at all what compassion meant until my brother died by suicide. It took his suicide for me to understand the meaning of compassion. I don't want other people to have to go through what I've been through to understand how important compassionate leadership is.

It's not possible to save or have a positive impact on every person on the planet. There are eight billion people on Earth, and not everyone is going to be a good fit for or want to learn from you, or even want your caring or compassion. Caring deeply and authentically for the people who do want to be around you, and who you want to be around, is half the equation. The other half is knowing when they aren't right for you or your values, and also when you aren't right for them.

As I was writing this chapter, I learned something new about this from my son. He seems to have been born with emotional intelligence. Honestly, I'm not sure where he got it—it must be from his mother. The other day, he came to me and told me that he wasn't going to be spending time with one particular group of his friends anymore. "I don't like the way they make me feel," he told me, "So I'm not going to hang out with them."

I am forty-three years old, and I'm still trying to figure that out. Hearing him talk about it reminded me how powerful this work is. Imagine if you could just choose to spend your time around people who give you energy, people who support you and share your values and make you feel good? Think how different that would feel every single day. To see my son exercising the emotional maturity to say, "This person doesn't make me feel good" inspired me to keep making those same kinds of choices for myself.

For entrepreneurs—as business leaders and as human beings—this goes back to core values. What are you all about? What do you want your life, and your business, to stand for and to mean? Where are you focusing? There's a saying in strategic planning that if everything is important, nothing is important. The same is true with people. You cannot invest in all of them. Your time, your energy, and your resources are limited.

I've had people on my team who I've invested in way too much. I sent them to trainings, tried to get them to grow and be better, and usually spent more time and energy on them than on the people who were already all-in with me. Holding onto a person who is not a fit is not doing them a service. It isn't kind or compassionate.

Part of saying goodbye, in other words, is saying goodbye to our unproductive mindsets. As entrepreneurs in particular, we need to say goodbye to the idea that we can do everything. One of my clients, for example, has a consistent, steady flow of brilliant ideas, so we have started having discussions around the question, "Which ones are you not going to do?"

It also means saying goodbye to the idea that we, the leaders, are the only ones with good ideas, the only ones able to drive the company forward. It means saying goodbye to being the smartest person in the room and embracing teamwork and other people's intelligence.

The incredible benefit of this, which I didn't understand until I started giving up some of my own mindsets and shifting toward compassion, is that saying goodbye to these other things also means saying goodbye to ninety-hour work weeks, unbearable stress and loneliness, and the feeling that you're missing the most important things in life while you deal with every single decision in your business.

A DIFFERENT FUTURE

Imagine what your life could look like instead. Imagine what it would feel like if you were surrounded by people who genuinely cared about you, and who you genuinely cared about. Imagine how that would impact your physical health, your emotional health, and your balance sheet. Imagine how hard those people would work to accomplish your shared vision.

Imagine if you shared this concept of compassion and caring with others on your team, or other entrepreneurs in your network, or the people you coach (which hopefully includes the leaders in your company), or your clients. It would spread outward—and come right back to you and support you.

Imagine learning this lesson before you lose someone and have to wonder what you could have done differently.

Without consistent application, though, we tend to revert to stasis and to our old patterns. Making these changes means getting a little better every week, every month, every quarter, and every year. Even a small effort, if it's consistent, will make an enormous difference.

One of my bosses in the Army was kind of a micromanager, and every time we had a meeting, the last thing he'd say as he was leaving the room was, "Just don't fuck it up." I have to admit, I was tempted to leave you with that. Compassion is critically important, much more so than anything he ever told us to do. Fortunately, there isn't really any way to mess it up. Just trying will get you a long way there.

If you see someone around you struggling, or suspect they might be having a hard time or thinking about suicide, please give them the resources I've listed at the end of the book.

And remember that it starts with having compassion for yourself. If you need help with this work—and you will—please find the resources and support that you need. Some of those resources are in this book. If you need more, I highly recommend seeking therapy or other support systems. Reach out and ask for what you need.

You can also head over to my website (calriley.com) for even more bonus materials, resources, and information about entrepreneurial compassion.

How you care for the people around you and for yourself will make more difference than any other investment you can make. It will repay you hundreds of times over, not only in business outcomes but in how you feel about your life, now and at the end when you look back on what mattered. It will compound and expand and ripple outward until you are surrounded by compassion and by people who genuinely repay your care for them.

All you have to do is start.

A TACSOP FOR COMPASSION

Authentic compassion isn't a step-by-step process. It's a lifelong journey of self-reflection and growth. But having a reference guide can help you stay focused on your compassion goals, reflect more effectively, and keep compassion in mind when life gets busy.

To guide your journey, I've created a TACSOP (Tactical Standard Operating Procedure): a pocket-sized reference to help guide your compassion practice on a day-to-day basis. Feel free to tear it out and take it with you, put it on your desk, or pin it to your wall as a reminder.

1. TAKE TIME TO REFLECT

Seeing and shifting old patterns of behavior requires self-reflection. Use these questions as an opportunity to reflect every day, to step back as often as possible and consider, "What are my core values, and what mindsets do I want to approach the world with?" Then look at your actions and be honest about whether you are acting according to those values and mindsets. "Am I treating people in a way that shows I genuinely care about them? Am I giving myself room to make mistakes and learn?" Without doubt, taking the time to reflect is the most powerful tool in your compassion toolbox.

2. LET GO OF CONTROL

As entrepreneurs, we tend to be driven and committed to achieving our goals. That's a positive attribute. But it can also get in the way of compassion—and success. When you find yourself doubling down on getting a certain outcome and not listening to alternatives, step back and figure out why you are so invested in that particular outcome.

3. GET CURIOUS

The best meetings I've ever had were the meetings where I spent lots of time listening and asking questions, not the ones where I gave a bunch of advice or tried to force people to do things my way. Step back from the leading role for a moment and ask questions instead to open up the conversation.

4. GIVE YOURSELF A BREAK

This compassion work shouldn't become one more area where you tell yourself you're failing. Pay attention to your self-talk. How often do you speak negatively about yourself? In particular, notice if that kind of language is coming out around other people. Driven leaders and entrepreneurs are often hardest on themselves, but that kind of thinking can affect how others see you, and how they think you see them. We can't be compassionate to others if we aren't compassionate to ourselves. Notice negative self-talk and ask, "Why is this happening today?"

5. ASSESS WHETHER PROBLEMS ARE TRUNK ISSUES OR LEAF ISSUES

I use the tree diagram (included in this book) to remind myself: some issues have the potential to put me out of business, and others are just day-to-day concerns. As the leader, it's my job to keep my focus on the trunk and root stuff, the big picture and potentially critical concerns. Everything else I can leave to my team. When you're in a meeting, ask yourself, "Is this a root or trunk problem, or is this a leaf someone else can take care of?"

6. INVEST IN PEOPLE AND RELATIONSHIPS

Investment in people takes a lot of forms, but part of compassionate leadership is investing in people financially, whether that's offering bonuses or giving people paid time off to take care of a family member. At the end of your life, you're going to remember the people you spent time with, not the contracts you earned or the business you brought in. Choose the people you want around you and then show them you care about them in a way they can recognize and feel. How much can you invest in your team? What will you get in return?

7. BE KIND, NOT (JUST) NICE

Being nice is...nice. But it's not always compassionate, and it's definitely not always good for your business. If someone on your team doesn't share your core values or is holding the rest of the team back, the most compassionate thing you can do is take the burden on yourself and let them go. Being kind often requires giving people honest feedback instead of being their friend. The people on your team already have buddies. What they need from you is leadership and the chance to accomplish something meaningful together. When you find yourself avoiding conflict or wanting to be everyone's friend, ask yourself what the team, and the business, need most from you.

8. PREPARE TO BE COMPASSIONATE— EVEN WHEN TIMES ARE TOUGH

Compassionate leadership doesn't happen by accident. The exercises in this book are a great place to start your compassion journey, and the best time to start is *before* things get so tough you have no other choice. My business survived COVID in part because we went ahead with bonuses we had already planned, and set aside money for, in the previous year. Not all preparation is financial (although that never hurts). Ask yourself how you'll handle tough conversations, how you will develop team members, and how you will make time for yourself, and track how the answers change over time.

9. LEAD FROM SHARED VALUES

Being compassionate just to get something in return isn't real compassion—but that doesn't mean you can't expect anything. Compassion shouldn't be a tactic or a manipulative tool. It's a core value, a driver that underlies everything else. If we as entrepreneurs lead from compassion, we can expect others on our teams to do the same. Hire people who are able and willing to share that value and to extend it to each other and to your clients, your vendors, and everyone else who is part of your company's success. Regularly check in with yourself: what are your values, and are you living and leading from them?

10. KEEP ASSESSING AND LEARNING

None of this happens overnight. It's a continuous process that relies on small gains and consistency. Ask, "How can I learn something new today, and how can I apply it with compassion?"

11. CELEBRATE SUCCESSES AND RECOGNIZE PROGRESS

Building a compassionate, caring team around yourself will be one of the greatest investments in your life. Take time to celebrate that.

12. GET HELP

If you or someone you know needs more support or is struggling, please take that as an opportunity to find help. The resources listed on the next page are a good place to start.

RESOURCES AND BEST PRACTICES FOR SUICIDE PREVENTION AND SUPPORT

YOU CAN HELP PREVENT SUICIDE: A GUIDE FOR ENTREPRENEURS AND LEADERS

Those of us who choose to lead choose responsibility. We are oriented to action. So how can you, as a leader, take action right now?

The good news is that you don't need to be perfect. You don't need to become a therapist. You just need to build your own capacity for compassion, and let it ripple outward from there.

Here's what you can do:

1. START WITH YOURSELF

Read this book. Complete all the exercises. Reflect on yourself and the legacy you want to leave in the world. Taking care of yourself isn't selfish; it's the baseline for taking care of others.

My goal is to prevent one hundred thousand suicides by creating one million compassionate leaders. You can be part of that by going to my website and signing the Entrepreneurial Compassion pledge (calriley.com).

2. SHARE WHAT YOU'VE LEARNED

Give this book to your leadership team. Use it to start a discussion about the culture you want to create and how to get there. I'm not telling you this to sell more books. All the profits from sales of this book go to suicide prevention nonprofits. Your leadership team drives the culture in your business. Getting them onboard with compassion is a powerful step in creating the ripple effect.

3. KNOW AND SHARE LIFE-SAVING RESOURCES

The list of resources and links at the back of this book is a great place to start. Help is available. There are amazing organizations that provide support and information. Sometimes, sharing a link can be enough to help someone get the support they need. You can find even more resources on my website at calriley.com.

4. KNOW THE WARNING SIGNS AND HOW TO RESPOND

Some of the most common warning signs of suicide are withdrawal from work, friends, or family, a loss of interest in things they used to enjoy, talking about helplessness of feeling trapped, hopeless, or like a burden. Sometimes people who are struggling with suicide have increased alcohol or drug use, dramatic mood changes, or reckless behavior. They might say, "I can't do this anymore" or "They would be better off without me."

Don't be afraid to speak directly with people. Asking, "Are you thinking about suicide?" doesn't plant the idea. It could save their life. The best thing you can do is listen without judgment, express care and concern, and connect them to resources. If someone is in immediate danger, stay with them and call 911, or take them to the nearest emergency room.

Don't let stigma or awkwardness keep you from helping someone. Struggling with suicide isn't anything to be ashamed of.

5. GIVE BACK

If you can, support life-saving organizations financially or by volunteering your time. Any of the organizations on the resources page of this book or on my website would be a good place to start.

RESOURCES

Struggling and asking for help are stigmatized in our culture, and especially in the military. Please share these resources with anyone who needs them—including yourself.

NEVER EVER GIVE UP!

Post these resources in your company's wellness resources, Slack channels, onboarding guides, and even in bathrooms. People often look for help silently before ever speaking up.

UNITED STATES
988 Suicide & Crisis Lifeline

Call or text 988 (24/7, free, confidential)
988lifeline.org

Crisis Text Line

Text HELLO to 741741 (24/7, anywhere in the US)

Veterans Crisis Line

Call or text 988, then press 1

Or chat: veteranscrisisline.net

*SAMHSA Treatment Locator (for therapy,
substance use, mental health support)*

findtreatment.gov

INTERNATIONAL

befrienders.org—International suicide prevention helplines
    iasp.info—International Association for Suicide Prevention

SUPPORT FOR VETERANS

Suicide prevention for veterans is available from the nonprofit
Roger at goroger.org/.

Veterans and Military Crisis Line

veteranscrisisline.net
    Confidential call, text, or chat for veterans and service
members.
    Visit veteranscrisisline.net/

COMMUNICATING ABOUT SUICIDE
WITH COMPASSION

**Using compassionate language to talk about suicide has real
consequences.** It reduces the stigma that still surrounds suicide
and creates the opportunity to talk about suicide as a mental
health crisis, not a crime or a sin. People are more likely to
seek help when they hear you speak respectfully about people

who are struggling because they can tell they won't be shamed or ostracized.

Compassionate language honors my brother's life, and the lives of others who have died by suicide, and recognizes and respects the grief of those left behind. Shifting the way we think and talk about suicide can impact policy, funding, and treatment and, ultimately, create more opportunity for prevention and care.

Language is a critical part of how we enact compassion for others, and it's especially important with a topic as sensitive and personal as suicide.

TERMS TO AVOID, AND WHAT TO SAY INSTEAD

"Committed suicide"

Why it's harmful: Saying someone "committed" suicide implies that suicide is a sin or a crime, the way we say that someone committed murder or adultery. Suicide isn't a moral failing. It's the result of mental illness, trauma, or pain.

What to say instead: Use the phrase, "died by suicide," which is neutral and focuses on the cause of death without blame or stigma—just like saying "died from cancer."

"Killed themselves" or "Took their own life"

Why it's harmful: Both of these phrases are harsh and jarring. The word "killed" implies violence, and it can be traumatizing for survivors. Suicide is complex and often results from months or years of suffering. These phrases reduce that complexity to one action.

What to say instead: Again, "died by suicide" centers the fact of death without dramatizing it or oversimplifying what led to it.

"Successful suicide" or "Completed suicide"

Why it's harmful: Suggesting that suicide is an accomplishment or a success can be hurtful to survivors and potentially even dangerous for people who are struggling with suicidal thoughts. These terms can also diminish the suffering of people who did not "succeed" in dying.

What to say instead: "Died by suicide." If you need to talk about attempts, say "survived a suicide attempt" or "lived through a suicide crisis."

Joking about suicide (such as "You should kill yourself" or "I'm going to kill myself" as a joke)

Why it's harmful: Suicide is devastating to individuals and families, and this kind of joking trivializes their pain, as well as the suffering experienced by people who die by suicide. It can also make true warning signs harder to see and discourage people from speaking up when they are struggling.

What to say instead: Treat all language about suicide with gravity and care. Create space for real conversations, not casual or sarcastic remarks.

ACKNOWLEDGEMENTS

I'd like to acknowledge my wife Amy for her loving support through the past thirteen years of our marriage, through the death of my brother and my father, and all the things we've been through together. I couldn't have done it without you. Thank you for being my rock, and I love you. Thank you to my son, Liam Riley, for teaching me what great leadership looks like and for your ability to do the hard things easily, and to my daughter, Jane Riley, for teaching me patience and how to be present, and for showing me how to be fun. To Feta for always being there for me. And thank you to my mom, for your ever-present love and support.

Thank you also to the many people who have helped me through this project: Dina Albukhary, for letting me bounce ideas off you, helping me fill the gaps, and showing me true resilience and grace at the same time; Gigi Crill, Tom and Chris Riley for always checking on me and being loving and supportive. My fellow officers and NCO brothers in arms who taught me what right looks like by example: Steve Cargill, Josh Cambria, Todd Kluttz, John Brostrom, Rob McQueen, Dan Chaves, Woody Crosby, Chris Swartz, and Garett Searle. For all of the amazing leaders I have had in my life: Dave Kaczmarek, Mark Leslie, David Fivecoat, and Andrew Rohling, to name only a few, what you taught me was incredibly valuable, and unfortunately a lot of it I just wasn't ready to learn until later in my life. My hope is that my readers are not as resistant to great leadership as I was!

Specifically Chris Tomasic, my wrestling coach, for instilling a sense of grit and determination, and at the same time having fun. Working hard and having a good time is something you modeled and still model well. My friend Jeremy Barefoot: thank you so much for your guidance and for reading this and helping me to get the confidence to write it. To my fellow entrepreneurs and leaders in the community: Dimitri Eliopoulos, Dave Rahe, Omar Palacios, Jon Barefoot, Audie Barefoot, Chris and Ana Quinn, Nicole Lindley, Curt Scott, Kim Mckeeman, Thomas Rhodes, Clint Robins, Paul Bauer, Freddie Kim, Quoc Tran, Morgan Gojanovich, Sonja Hopson, Joe Maioriello, Mark Pembleton, Jason Barfield, Emily Cambria, Paige Patterson, John Patterson, Jason Sewell, Adam Chrisco, Dino Skerlos, Cobey Mandarino, Jim Freeman, Dave and Emily Brown, Sanjay Das, Brian Dumont, Mike Anderson, Zac Davenport, Jim Harris, Arturo Marshawn, Mike Hensley, Marissa Pratt, Scott Alexander, Brian Cox, Ryan Garner, Patrick Gocke, Robert Mckenzie, Moss Withers, Ryan Thomsen, Jeff Walters. To my earliest coaching clients who are no longer with me: sorry for the poor performance and for not knowing what I didn't know, and thank you for all you taught me! I probably learned more from you than you did from me.

To my cousins Zach Wineburg and Mark Merkel for always

being there and for being open to my insane schedule. Nicole Marsh, this book wouldn't exist without your support! To my friends Stephen Loicanno, Leo Lucisano, Nate Foust, Jimmy Philbin, and Ryan Weiggle. For my fellow business coaches out there: Rodney Mueller, Bob Faoderson, Dan Singer, John Gross, Pete Winne, Dean Durbin, Jim Coyle, JBS, Scott Rusniak, Mark Odonnel (both of you!), Jen Couldry, Ray Salinas, Dick Schultz, and Steve King.

For Gino Wickman for creating such an amazing thing in founding EOS. I am so lucky I am part of this amazing community!

And finally, for all of my amazing teammates at Riley Contracting Group: I wouldn't have a company without such amazing people, and you all make it an absolute pleasure to be an entrepreneur. All of you have done so much to make us a great organization. Specifically, Luis Cardneas for your always positive attitude and your ability to charm anyone. I am so grateful that I get to see you grow in this next chapter. Eric Garbarino, for your sense of humor and for always finding a way to get the job done. Jim Herthum for your faith and trust in me, Lenny Lynch for helping me to grow into a real leader and for your wisdom, Britni Holman for your true and tireless dedication, Rob Bromley for your dedication, wisdom and for teaching me all about construction and business, Brian Relay for your dedication to the legacy of this company and for helping us to keep our amazing reputation, Charlie Quinn for your ability to charm anyone and at the same time effortlessly (or at least it looks that way) get the projects done, Marico "Reese" Clark for your ability to find a way, Alex Egresists for your sense of humor and dedication (always with a smile on your face), Darrell Kirby for your dedication and commitment to finding a way. To Gary Patrowicz, for your hard work: you told me on your first day that you just want to work, and man, do you work hard. Rick Armstrong for everything, for being you, and for being one of the guys who is setting the standard of what a "Riley Job" looks like. Shawn Anthony and Dominique Montgomery for your dedication and experience, and Meagan Carothers for being so dedicated and always learning. Florida Hughes, for everything you do: you are a true utility player. I appreciate having all of you on my team and seeing you grow.

I know I've forgotten people. If so, forgive me, but know that if I know you, you've had an incredible impact on my life.

ABOUT THE AUTHOR

CAL RILEY is an entrepreneur, investor, and business coach who loves to spend time with his wife Amy, his children Liam and Jane, and his dog Feta. Cal spent a decade fighting the Global War on Terror in the Army, first as an Infantry officer and then in Special Operations. After leading men in combat, Cal transitioned to the private sector and became an entrepreneur and business coach. Using his hard-earned lessons from the battlefield and in the boardroom, Cal coaches the best entrepreneurs and helps them to get even better.

www.ingramcontent.com/pod-product-compliance
Lightning Source LLC
Chambersburg PA
CBHW030504210326
41597CB00013B/783